COMPLETE CAKE
DECORATING

Progressing from Easy to Experienced to Expert, this collection of beautifully embellished cakes, cupcakes and cookies offers over 30 exquisite creations for all those special occasions, including weddings, birthdays and christenings. Step-by-step instructions and photographs, together with a comprehensive section of techniques, offer all that you need to know to turn a simple cake into a work of art.

With every recipe triple-tested® for perfect results, this excellent cookbook is sure to be one of the best-loved on your kitchen bookshelf. To discover the rest of our range of cookbooks, together with our unrivalled selection of creative kitchenware, visit one of our friendly Lakeland stores or shop online at www.lakeland.co.uk.

COMPLETE CAKE
DECORATING

LAKELAND

Lakeland and Bauer Media Ltd hereby exclude all liability to the extent permitted by law for any errors or omission in this book and for any loss, damage or expense (whether direct or indirect) suffered by a third party relying on any information contained in this book.

This book was created in 2013 for Lakeland by AWW Books, an imprint of Octopus Publishing Group Ltd, based on materials licensed to it by Bauer Media Books, Sydney.

Bauer Media Limited
54 Park St, Sydney
GPO Box 4088, Sydney, NSW 2001
www.awwcookbooks.com.au

MEDIA GROUP

OCTOPUS PUBLISHING GROUP
Design – Chris Bell
Food Director – Pamela Clark

Published for Lakeland in the United Kingdom by Octopus Publishing Group Limited

Endeavour House
189 Shaftesbury Avenue
London WC2H 8JY
United Kingdom
phone + 44 (0) 207 632 5400;
fax + 44 (0) 207 632 5405
aww@octopusbooks.co.uk;
www.octopusbooks.co.uk
www.australian-womens-weekly.com

Printed and bound in China

A catalogue record for this book is available from the British Library.

ISBN 978-1-909770-05-8

The Department of Health advises that eggs should not be consumed raw. This book contains some dishes made with raw or lightly cooked eggs. It is prudent for vulnerable people such as pregnant and nursing mothers, invalids, the elderly, babies and young children to avoid uncooked or lightly cooked dishes made with eggs. Once prepared, these dishes should be kept refrigerated and used promptly.

This book also includes dishes made with nuts and nut derivatives. It is advisable for those with known allergic reactions to nuts and nut derivatives and those who may be potentially vulnerable to these allergies, such as pregnant and nursing mothers, invalids, the elderly, babies and children to avoid dishes made with nuts and nut oils. It is also prudent to check the labels of pre-prepared ingredients for the possible inclusion of nut derivatives.

Some of the recipes in this book have appeared in other publications.

CONTENTS

EQUIPMENT

1

2

3

4

5

6

7

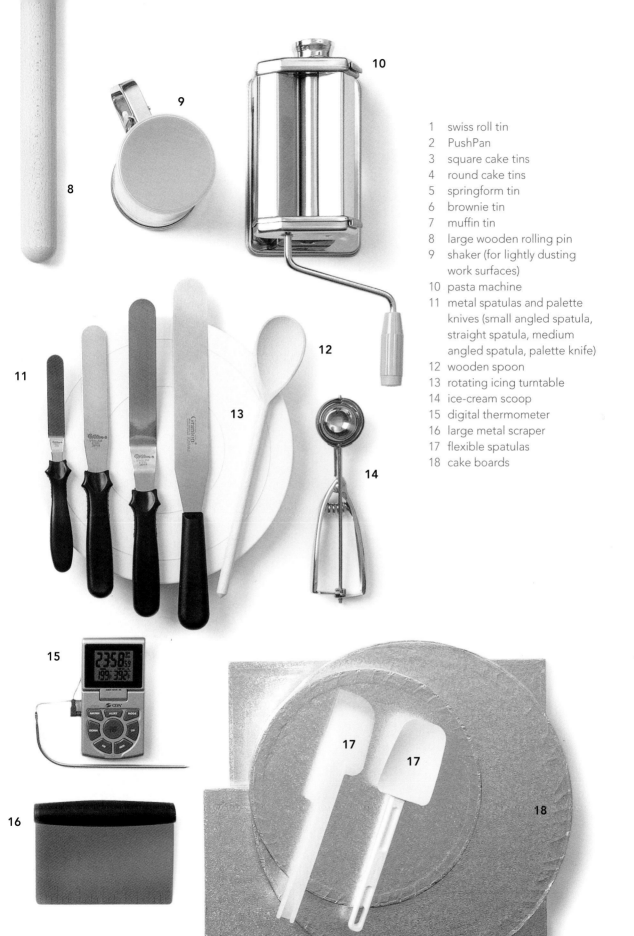

1 swiss roll tin
2 PushPan
3 square cake tins
4 round cake tins
5 springform tin
6 brownie tin
7 muffin tin
8 large wooden rolling pin
9 shaker (for lightly dusting work surfaces)
10 pasta machine
11 metal spatulas and palette knives (small angled spatula, straight spatula, medium angled spatula, palette knife)
12 wooden spoon
13 rotating icing turntable
14 ice-cream scoop
15 digital thermometer
16 large metal scraper
17 flexible spatulas
18 cake boards

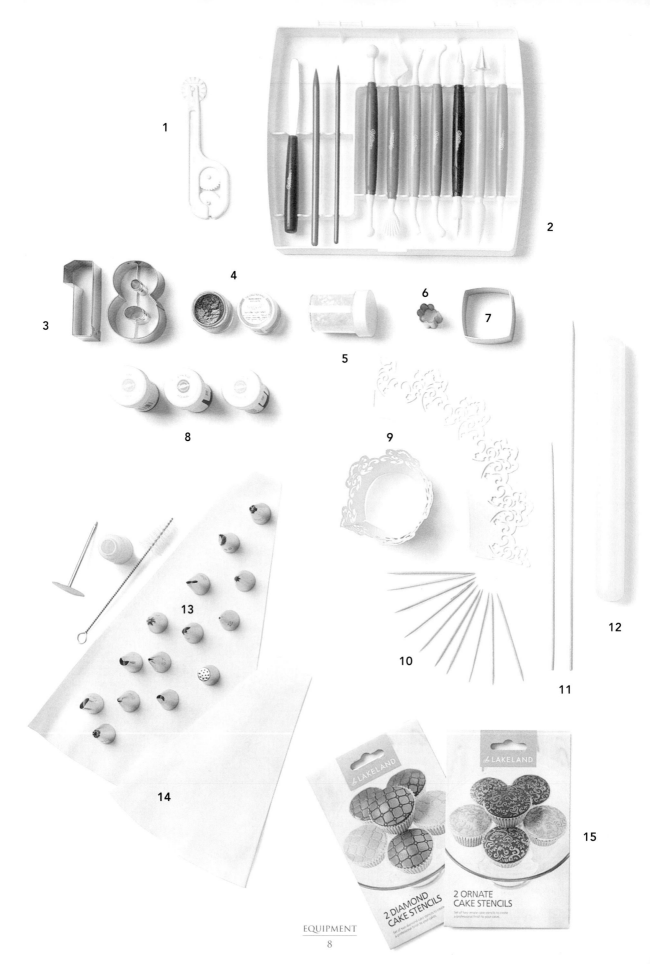

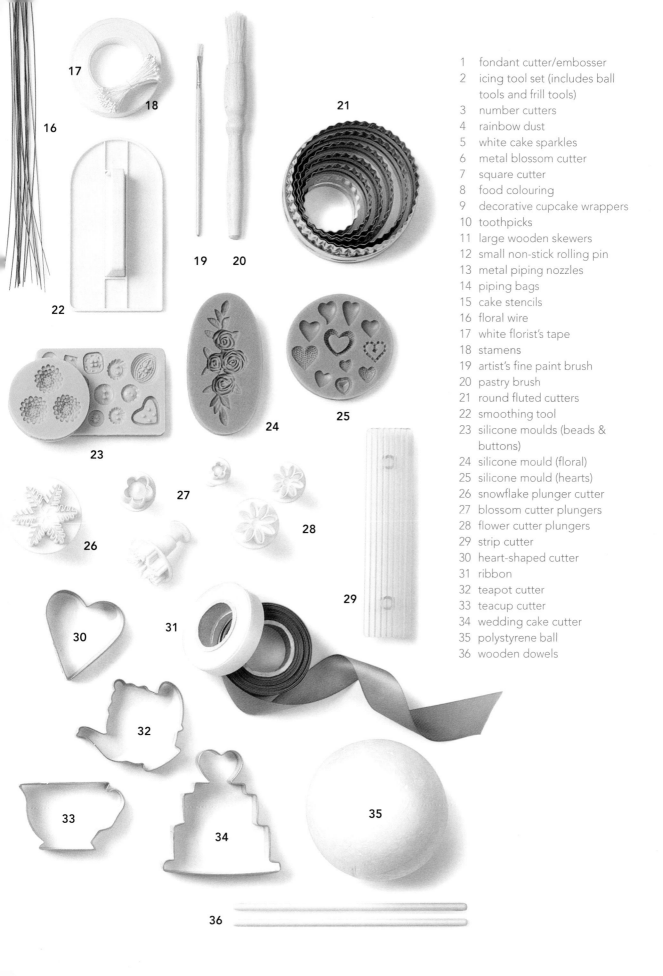

1 fondant cutter/embosser
2 icing tool set (includes ball tools and frill tools)
3 number cutters
4 rainbow dust
5 white cake sparkles
6 metal blossom cutter
7 square cutter
8 food colouring
9 decorative cupcake wrappers
10 toothpicks
11 large wooden skewers
12 small non-stick rolling pin
13 metal piping nozzles
14 piping bags
15 cake stencils
16 floral wire
17 white florist's tape
18 stamens
19 artist's fine paint brush
20 pastry brush
21 round fluted cutters
22 smoothing tool
23 silicone moulds (beads & buttons)
24 silicone mould (floral)
25 silicone mould (hearts)
26 snowflake plunger cutter
27 blossom cutter plungers
28 flower cutter plungers
29 strip cutter
30 heart-shaped cutter
31 ribbon
32 teapot cutter
33 teacup cutter
34 wedding cake cutter
35 polystyrene ball
36 wooden dowels

THE CAKES

EASY

CHOCOLATE BOX

equipment
20cm square cake board (page 137)
medium metal spatula
craft glue
cheese planer

cake
deep 15cm square cake of choice (pages 102–117)

decorations
1 quantity white chocolate ganache (page 126)
250g white chocolate Melts
golden yellow food colouring
1.5m wide ribbon
540g blocks white eating chocolate

1 Trim cake (page 120); secure cake to board (page 120). Spread cake all over with ganache.
2 Cut baking parchment into four strips measuring 10cm x 16cm. Melt chocolate Melts in heatproof bowl over medium saucepan of simmering water (don't let water touch base of bowl). Remove from heat; tint chocolate with a little yellow colouring.
3 Using spatula, spread chocolate evenly over the baking-parchment strips. Leave chocolate to set for a few minutes, then carefully pick up parchment and move to another sheet of baking parchment (this neatens the edges) (*step 1*). Stand about 5 minutes or until chocolate sets.
4 Peel baking parchment away from chocolate panels (*step 2*); press panels onto sides of cake. Wrap ribbon around panels;

secure ends with glue. Make bow (page 138); secure over ribbon with glue.
5 Place one block of chocolate upside down on work top. Place your hand on the chocolate to warm it slightly. Drag a sharp cheese planer over the chocolate to make curls (*step 3*). Repeat with remaining chocolate to make enough curls to cover and fill the top of the chocolate box. Fill box with chocolate curls.

tips We found a cheese planer an easy and effective way of making large chocolate curls.
• The box panels can be completed at least one week before they're needed; store at a cool room temperature.
• You can use this recipe as a guide to make the boxes smaller or larger.

Step 1 To make chocolate panels, spread melted chocolate over four strips of baking parchment. When starting to set, lift onto clean baking parchment.

Step 2 Stand the chocolate at room temperature until it's set. Turn the chocolate over, peel away baking parchment. Position panels around cake.

Step 3 Place chocolate upside down on bench. Rub your hand over chocolate to warm slightly; drag cheese planer over chocolate for curls.

QUILTED WEDDING CAKE COOKIES

equipment
oven trays
10cm x 10.5cm wedding cake
    cutter
pastry brush
non-stick rolling pin
diamond design cake stencil
fine artist's paint brush
tweezers

cookies
125g butter, at room
    temperature
1 teaspoon vanilla extract
150g caster sugar
2 eggs, at room temperature
200g self-raising flour
150g plain flour

decorations
500g ready-made white icing
cornflour
1 egg white, beaten lightly
2 tablespoons tiny silver cachous

1 Beat butter, extract and sugar in small bowl with electric mixer only until combined. Beat in eggs, one at a time; beat only until combined.
2 Transfer mixture to large bowl. Stir in sifted flours, in two batches; mix to a soft dough. Knead dough on floured surface until smooth, cover; refrigerate 30 minutes.
3 Preheat oven to 180°C. Grease oven trays; line trays with baking parchment.
4 Roll dough, in batches, between sheets of baking parchment until 5mm thick. Using wedding cake cutter, cut 18 shapes, re-rolling dough as necessary (*step 1*). Place shapes, about 3cm apart, on trays. Bake about 10 minutes or until cookies are browned lightly.
5 Stand cookies on trays 5 minutes; transfer onto wire racks to cool.
6 Knead ready-made icing on surface dusted with a little

cornflour until icing loses its stickiness. Roll icing on cornfloured surface to a 3mm thickness. Position diamond stencil on icing. Roll over stencil with rolling pin to make a quilted pattern. Using the wedding cake cutter, cut shape from icing; re-roll icing as necessary. Cover icing shapes with cling film (*step 2*).
7 Working with one cookie at a time, brush the top of the cookie with egg white. Lift icing shapes onto cookies.
8 Dip paint brush into water, wipe brush almost dry, dab onto one join in the quilted pattern; use tweezers to position cachous on join (*step 3*). Repeat with remaining cachous; stand cookies until set.

makes 18
tip Completed cookies can be made up to 4 weeks ahead; store in an airtight container.

Step 1 Roll out cookie dough between sheets of baking parchment until 5mm thick. Using the wedding cake cutter, cut out 18 shapes. Bake cookies.

Step 2 Position stencil on icing. Roll over stencil with rolling pin to make a quilted pattern. Cut wedding cake shape from icing. Brush cookies with egg white and top with icing shape.

Step 3 Dip paint brush into water, wipe brush until almost dry. Lightly dab one join at a time with brush then position cachous on join.

SUGAR CONFETTI CUPCAKES

equipment
12 plain white paper cases
large piping bag
1cm plain piping tube

cake
1 quantity cupcake mixture of
  choice (pages 102–117)
jam of choice

decorations
12 plain decorative cupcake
  wrappers
1½ quantities white chocolate
  ganache (page 126), whipped
  (see *step 1*)
2 tablespoons sugar confetti

1 Divide cupcake mixture into paper cases; bake cupcakes according to recipe. Stand cakes in tin 5 minutes; turn top-side up onto wire rack to cool.
2 Using a small pointed knife or cupcake corer, cut a small cavity in the cake top. Fill cavity with jam; use a flavour that will complement the cake. Place cakes into cupcake wrappers.
3 Fit piping bag with tube; half-fill bag with ganache. Pipe swirls of ganache on top of each cake (*step 3*). Sprinkle ganache with sugar confetti.

makes 12
tips Cupcakes stale quickly, so it's best to use a fruit or mud cake for the best keeping qualities.
• The cakes can be made and frozen for about 3 months.
• Choose the cake you like, then a type of jam, or a thick fruit purée, to match the cake. For example, any berry jam or purée goes well with a chocolate cake.
• Make sure you cover the tops of the cakes with the ganache; it will keep them sealed and fresh for a day or two.
• Completed cakes should be stored in a cool place.
• Sprinkle sugar confetti over ganache up to half a day before the cupcakes are to be served.

Step 1 Whip the white chocolate ganache in a small bowl with an electric mixer until the ganache is smooth and thick enough to pipe.

Step 2 Cut a small cavity in the cake top using a small pointed vegetable knife. Fill cavity with jam; use a flavour that will complement the cake.

Step 3 Half-fill the piping bag with whipped ganache. Start piping from the centre of the cake, covering the top of each cake to make a large swirl.

POLKA DOTS & STRIPES

equipment
25cm round cake tins
25cm round cake board (page 137)
non-stick rolling pin
smoothing tools
2cm, 1.5cm and 1cm round cutters
fine artist's paint brush

cake
4 x 500g packets sponge cake mix
golden yellow, rose pink, mauve and leaf green food colourings

decorations
4 quantities white chocolate ganache (page 126)
800g ready-made white icing
cornflour

1 Preheat oven to 180°C. Grease cake tins; line base with baking parchment.

2 Make one cake mix according to packet directions. Tint mixture with yellow colouring, spread into tin, bake cake about 30 minutes. Stand cake in tin 5 minutes; turn top-side up onto wire rack to cool. Repeat with remaining cake mixes and pink, mauve and green colouring. Trim cakes level (page 120), if necessary.

3 Secure one cake to board with a little ganache; top with remaining cakes using about 145g of the ganache between each layer. Spread cake evenly all over with remaining ganache (page 126).

4 Knead 600g ready-made icing on surface dusted with a little cornflour until icing loses its stickiness. Roll icing on cornfloured surface until large enough to cover cake. Using rolling pin, lift icing onto cake; smooth with hands then smoothing tools. Trim icing neatly around base of cake.

5 Knead remaining icing on surface dusted with cornflour until smooth. Divide into four equal portions; colour pale pink, green, mauve and yellow. Keep each enclosed in cling film while not using. Roll one colour out to 1mm thick. Using cutters, cut rounds from icing, re-rolling icing as necessary (step 1). Repeat with remaining icings. Brush backs of dots sparingly with water (step 2); position dots on cake (step 3). Cut some dots in half to decorate around bottom of cake. Dry cake overnight.

tips We used the end of a 1cm piping tube to cut out the smallest dots.
• We used packet cake mixes – the cake will keep and cut well and has a fine texture. If you want to make your own cake, we suggest the deep 25cm round butter cake recipe on page 102. One quantity of this recipe will be equivalent in volume to one packet of cake mix.

Step 1 Using all three cutters, cut out rounds from all four colours of icing. Keep the icings you're not using airtight by wrapping in cling film.

Step 2 Brush backs of dots lightly with water and randomly position on cake. Don't use too much water or the dots will slip and slide off.

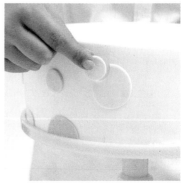

Step 3 Position half-dots around base of the cake. Position the dots before they dry so they will more readily take on the contour of the cake.

BROWNIE & BLONDIE MINI WEDDING CAKES

equipment
2 x 23cm x 33cm cm swiss roll
  tins
5cm, 3.5cm and 2.5cm round
  cutters
paper piping bag (page 131)

dark chocolate brownie
300g dark eating chocolate
185g butter
25g cocoa powder
220g light brown sugar
165g caster sugar
2 teaspoons vanilla extract
4 eggs
225g plain flour

white chocolate blondie
300g white eating chocolate
185g butter
220g caster sugar
3 eggs
185g plain flour
110g self-raising flour

decorations
½ quantity dark chocolate
  ganache (page 126)
2 tablespoons icing sugar
½ teaspoon edible silver glitter

1 Preheat oven to 150°C. Grease swiss roll tins; line base and long sides with baking parchment.
2 Make dark chocolate brownie and white chocolate blondie.
3 Turn blondie and brownie onto board, trim all sides of both cakes (*step 1*).
4 Using all of the cutters, cut out 12 rounds of each size from both the brownie and the blondie (*step 2*).
5 Make three-tier stacks, alternating rounds of brownies and blondies; secure each tier with ganache (*step 3*).
6 Dust stacks with combined sifted icing sugar and glitter before serving.

dark chocolate brownie Break chocolate into medium saucepan, add chopped butter and sifted cocoa; stir over low heat until smooth. Cool until just warmed; whisk in sugars, extract, eggs and sifted flour. Spread mixture into one swiss roll tin. Bake about 35 minutes. Cool in tin.

white chocolate blondie Break chocolate into medium saucepan, add chopped butter; stir over low heat until smooth. Cool until just warmed; whisk in sugar, eggs and sifted flours. Spread mixture into second swiss roll tin. Bake about 35 minutes. Cool in tin.

makes 24
tips The cakes will keep for about 3 days in an airtight container at a cool room temperature. Dust the cakes with sifted icing sugar and glitter just before serving.

Step 1 Turn brownie onto a cutting board. Using a long, sharp serrated knife, trim all sides. Repeat with the blondie.

Step 2 Using the three different-sized round cutters, cut out 12 rounds of each size from both the brownie and the blondie.

Step 3 Make three-tier stacks, alternating rounds of brownie and blondie. Pipe a dab of chocolate ganache onto tiers to secure.

BRIGHT LITTLE JELLY BEAN CAKES

equipment
3 x 10cm round cardboard cake
  boards (page 137)
2 x 12cm round cake boards
  (page 137)
6 wooden skewers

cake
3 x deep 10cm round cakes of
  choice (pages 102–117)
2 x deep 12cm round cakes of
  choice (pages 102–117)

decorations
2 quantities butter cream (page
  124)
rose pink, leaf green and yellow
  food colouring
200g jelly beans, approximately,
  in colours to match butter
  cream

1 Divide butter cream evenly into
three medium bowls; tint pink,
green and yellow.
2 Trim cakes (page 120). Secure
the three 10cm cakes to the 10cm
boards with a little butter cream
(page 120) (*step 1*). Secure the
two 12cm cakes to the 12cm
boards.
3 Push 3 trimmed skewers into
both 12cm cakes to support the
top tiers (*step 2*) (page 134).
4 Secure two of the 10cm cakes
to the 12cm cakes (page 135)
(*step 3*). You will have 2 x two-
tiered cakes and 1 x one-tier cake.
5 Spread cakes all over with
butter cream. Using picture as a
guide, decorate cakes with jelly
beans to match the colours of the
butter cream.

makes 3 cakes
tip Use ganache instead of
butter cream, if you prefer. Once
the cakes are covered in butter
cream or ganache, they will keep
for about a week at a cool room
temperature.
• The jelly beans can be placed
on the cakes as soon as the butter
cream has been applied.

*Step 1 Secure the three 10cm
cakes to the 10cm boards with
a little butter cream. Secure the
two 12cm cakes to the 12cm
boards.*

*Step 2 Using a sharp serrated
knife, trim skewers to the height
of the cake. Push skewers into
the largest cakes to support the
top tiers.*

*Step 3 Once all cakes are on
boards, secure two of the smaller
cakes onto the larger cakes with
a little of the butter cream.*

EMBOSSED LACE CUPCAKES

equipment
12 plain white paper cases
ornate cake stencil
7cm round cutter
non-stick rolling pin
new large soft-bristled brush

cake
1 quantity cupcake mixture of
   choice (pages 102–117)

decorations
1 quantity white chocolate
   ganache (page 126)
500g ready-made white icing
cornflour
12 fancy cupcake wrappers
edible white shimmer

1 Divide cupcake mixture into
paper cases; bake cupcakes
according to recipe. Stand cakes
in tin 5 minutes; turn top-side up
onto wire rack to cool.
2 Spread tops of cakes evenly
all over with ganache.
3 Knead ready-made icing
on surface dusted with a little
cornflour until icing loses
its stickiness. Roll icing on
cornfloured surface until about
5mm thick (*step 1*).
4 Place stencil on top of icing.
With the rolling pin, apply a light
pressure while rolling over the
stencil design (*step 2*). Carefully
remove stencil and repeat to
cover icing with the design
(*step 3*). Using cutter, cut out 12
rounds from icing; carefully place
rounds on cakes without touching
the embossed pattern. Knead
and re-roll the icing and cut out
more rounds as needed.

5 Carefully place cakes into
cupcake wrappers. Dip brush
into shimmer; brush lightly over
embossed pattern.

makes 12
tips If you like, choose a few
different cake recipes, so you get
a variety of cakes.
• The ganache and ready-made
icing covering will keep the cakes
fresh for a few days if stored in a
cool place.
• Apply the shimmer to the icing
a few hours before serving; a soft-
bristled make-up brush is ideal for
doing this.

Step 1 *Roll the ready-made
soft icing into a 5mm thickness
on a surface lightly dusted with
cornflour.*

Step 2 *Place stencil on icing
and use rolling pin with a light
pressure to apply pattern.*

Step 3 *Slowly and carefully
remove stencil from the patterned
icing to prevent damaging the
pattern.*

LEMON MERINGUE CUPCAKES

equipment
12 straight-sided fancy paper
  cases
oven tray
large piping bag
2cm plain piping tube
craft glue

cake
1 quantity cupcake mixture of
  choice (pages 102–117)

meringues
2 egg whites
110g caster sugar
lemon yellow food colouring

decorations
320g lemon curd
3m narrow ribbon

1 Divide cupcake mixture into paper cases; bake cupcakes according to recipe. Stand cakes in tin 5 minutes; turn top-side up onto wire rack to cool.
2 Reduce oven temperature to 100°C. Grease and line oven tray with baking parchment (see tips).
3 To make meringues, beat egg whites and sugar in small bowl with electric mixer until sugar is dissolved and mixture is thick and glossy. Tint meringue pale yellow.
4 Fit piping bag with tube, half-fill bag with meringue; pipe 12 meringues, with bases 5cm wide, onto oven tray, about 5cm apart, refilling bag as necessary (*step 1*). Bake meringues about 45 minutes or until dry to touch. Cool in oven with door ajar.
5 Trim tops from cakes so the tops are flat and 1cm below the top of the paper cases. Spread

one tablespoon of lemon curd over each cake to completely cover the surface of the cake. Top cakes with meringues (*step 2*).
6 Position a length of ribbon around each cake; secure ends with glue. Use ribbon to make bows (page 138); secure over joins with glue (*step 3*).

makes 12
tips Use a 5cm round cutter to draw circles on baking parchment about 5cm apart. Turn the paper over and use circles as a guide to pipe the meringues.
• Cakes can be frozen for up to 3 months. Meringues can be made a week ahead and stored in an airtight container at a cool room temperature. Assemble the cakes up to a day before needed.

Step 1 Pipe meringues onto tray. If you like, draw 5cm circles, 5cm apart, on the baking parchment as a guide; turn parchment over before piping.

Step 2 Trim tops from the cakes so they are about 1cm below the top of the paper cases to make room and top with the lemon curd and meringue.

Step 3 Using craft glue, secure a length of ribbon around the cake cases. Cover the ends of the ribbon with small bows secured with glue.

MANGO ROSE CHEESECAKES

equipment
4 x 10cm (closed) springform
  cake tins

cheesecake
250g cream cheese
1 x 450g unfilled store-bought
  sponge slab (13cm x 18cm)
1 teaspoon powdered gelatine
2 tablespoons lime juice
2 teaspoons finely grated lime
  rind
55g caster sugar
250ml pouring cream

decoration
2 medium firm ripe mangoes
  (860g)

1 Have cream cheese at room temperature.
2 Split sponge cake into two even layers. Using base of one springform tin as a guide, cut out four rounds of sponge (*step 1*). Use scraps of sponge to patch and complete rounds, as necessary.
3 Line base and sides of springform tins with baking parchment. Place sponge rounds into tins.
4 To make cheesecake: Sprinkle gelatine over juice in small heatproof jug. Stand 5 minutes then place jug in small saucepan of simmering water, stir until gelatine is dissolved. Cool 5 minutes.
5 Beat cream cheese, rind and sugar in small bowl with electric mixer until smooth; beat in cream.

Stir in gelatine mixture.
6 Divide cream cheese mixture evenly between tins; level tops. Refrigerate overnight.
7 Remove cheesecakes from tins, place on serving plates. Slice mango into 3mm thick slices (*step 2*). Starting from the centre of each cheesecake, and using small pieces of mango first, arrange slices into a rose shape (*step 3*).

makes 4
tips We used a plain store-bought sponge for this recipe. but you can make your own, if you like.
• You can use 10cm PushPans instead of the springform cake tins. There is no need to line the base and sides of PushPans with baking parchment.

Step 1 *Using base of one of the springform tins, cut out two sponge rounds close to the edge. Use scraps to complete second sponge round.*

Step 2 *You need mangoes that are ripe, but firm enough to slice thinly. Peel mangoes, remove cheeks from seed, and then slice the cheeks.*

Step 3 *Starting from the centre of the cheesecake, and using small slices of mango for the bud, arrange mango slices into a rose shape.*

PINK VELVET MACAROON CAKE

equipment
22cm and 15cm deep round cake tins
30cm and 15cm round cake boards (page 137)
medium offset metal spatula
3 wooden skewers

cake
250g butter, at room temperature
4 eggs, at room temperature
2 teaspoons vanilla extract
660g caster sugar
450g plain flour
50g cornflour
35g cocoa powder
500ml buttermilk
2 tablespoons rose pink food colouring
2 teaspoons white vinegar
2 teaspoons bicarbonate of soda

cream cheese frosting
185g butter
500g cream cheese
2 tablespoons strained lemon juice
1.4kg icing sugar

decorations
36 small french macaroons

1 Preheat oven to 180°C. Grease and line cake tins (page 136).
2 To make cake, beat butter, eggs, extract and sugar in small bowl with electric mixer until light and fluffy. Transfer mixture to large bowl; stir in sifted flour, cornflour and cocoa, and combined buttermilk and colouring in two batches.
3 Combine vinegar and soda in small bowl; allow to fizz, then fold into cake mixture. Divide mixture between tins. Bake large cake about 1 hour 20 minutes and small cake about 1 hour.
4 Stand cakes in tins 10 minutes before turning top-side up onto wire racks to cool. Wrap cooled cakes in cling film, freeze about 40 minutes or until cakes are firm.
5 Make cream cheese frosting.
6 Trim cakes (page 120). Split large cake into three even layers (step 1). Secure one layer to largest board with a little frosting. Top with remaining layers using about 75g of the frosting between each layer.

7 Split smaller cake into three even layers. Secure one layer to small board with a little frosting. Top with the remaining layers using about 75g of the frosting between each layer. Use spatula to spread remaining frosting over top and sides of both cakes.
8 Push trimmed skewers into large cake to support the top tier (page 134). Position small cake on large cake. Smooth frosting with spatula.
9 Gently twist each macaroon to separate into two halves (step 2); press the macaroon halves around the sides of both cakes before the frosting sets (step 3).

cream cheese frosting Have butter and cream cheese at room temperature. Beat butter, cream cheese and juice in large bowl with electric mixer until light and fluffy. Gradually beat in sifted icing sugar until frosting is smooth.

tip You can buy ready-made macaroons or make your own.

Step 1 Wrap cakes in cling film and freeze for about 40 minutes or until the cakes are firm. Split each cake into three even layers.

Step 2 Gently twist macaroons to separate the halves or, if firmly stuck, carefully cut through the centre with a small sharp knife.

Step 3 Gently press the macaroon halves around the sides of both cakes. Arrange the in any colour combination you like.

COCONUT DREAM CREAM CAKE

equipment
45cm, 25cm, 20cm, 15cm and
  10cm round cake boards (page
  137)
12 wooden skewers
small offset metal spatula

cake
deep 30cm, 25cm, 20cm, 15cm
  and 10cm round cakes of
  choice (pages 102–117)

decorations
3 quantities white chocolate
  ganache (page 126)
white food colouring
1.8kg ball-shaped coconut
  chocolates

1 Trim cakes (page 120). Secure largest cake to the largest board (page 120). Secure the remaining cakes to the same-sized boards.
2 Push three trimmed skewers into centre of each cake, except the smallest cake, to support the next tier (page 134).
3 Assemble cakes, securing each tier to the tier below (page 135).
4 Beat ganache in large bowl with electric mixer *(step 1)*. Beat in enough white colouring to match the colour of the ganache to the coconut chocolates. Spread cake all over with ganache *(step 2)*.
5 Cut chocolates in half *(step 3)*, press cut-sides around each cake, starting at the bottom of the largest cake.

tips The cake can be completed a day ahead. It will be fine kept in a cool place.
• Instead of making the ganache, you could buy three 453g tubs of vanilla frosting to cover this cake.

Step 1 *Beat ganache in large bowl with electric mixer. Use white colouring to match the colour of the ganache to the chocolates.*

Step 2 *Using a small metal spatula, spread ganache evenly all over the stacked cake to make the cake airtight.*

Step 3 *Using a sharp knife, cut coconut chocolates in half. Starting from the bottom of the cake, push cut sides of chocolates onto ganache.*

HEARTS & BOWS FOREVER

equipment
non-stick rolling pin
3cm heart cutter
22cm round cake board (page 137)
small offset metal spatula

cake
2 x deep 18cm round cakes of choice (pages 102–117)

decorations
150g ready-made white icing
cornflour
lemon yellow food colouring
1½ quantities white chocolate ganache (page 126)
1m wide ribbon

1 Knead ready-made icing on surface dusted with a little cornflour until icing loses its stickiness. Tint icing yellow with colouring. Roll icing out on cornfloured surface into 3mm thickness.
2 Using cutter, cut out about 70 heart shapes from icing, re-rolling scraps as necessary (*step 1*). Place hearts on baking-parchment-lined tray for about 3 hours, or until hearts are firm, but not dried out or hard.
3 Trim cakes (page 120). Secure one cake to board (page 120); top with remaining cake, joining cakes with a little ganache (page 134).
4 Beat remaining ganache in small bowl with electric mixer until light and fluffy.

5 Using spatula, spread ganache all over cake (*step 2*).
6 Starting from the bottom of the cake, press heart shapes onto ganache in rows before the ganache sets (*step 3*).
7 Just before serving, decorate the top of the cake with a bow made from the ribbon (page 138).

tips If you prefer, use butter cream instead of ganache; both will keep the cake airtight and fresh for at least a week in a cool room.

Step 1 Cut out 70 heart shapes from the ready-made icing; place on a baking-parchment-lined tray until firm, but not dried out or hard.

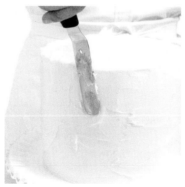

Step 2 Secure one cake to board; join remaining cake to bottom cake with ganache. Spread cake evenly all over with remaining ganache.

Step 3 Starting from the bottom of the cake, gently press the heart shapes in rows around the cake. Do this before the ganache sets.

LAST-MINUTE CAKE WITH FRESH FLOWERS

equipment
30cm, 20cm and 15cm round
   cake boards (page 137)
6 wooden skewers
small offset metal spatula

cake
deep 25cm, 20cm and 15cm
   round cakes of choice (pages
   102–117)

decorations
2 quantities fluffy frosting (page
   125) (see tips)
fresh organic flowers
white florist's tape

1 Trim cakes (page 120). Secure
large cake to largest board;
secure remaining cakes to same-
sized boards (page 120).
2 Push three trimmed skewers
into centre of large and medium
cakes to support the top tiers
(page 134). Secure medium cake
on top of large cake; secure small
cake on top of medium cake
(page 135).
3 Make fluffy frosting (*step 1*).
4 Working quickly, spread
frosting all over cake (*step 2*).
5 Trim then wrap flower stems in
florist's tape. Position flowers on
top of cake (*step 3*).

tips Make the frosting after you
have stacked and secured the
cakes; you need to work quickly
once the frosting is ready as it
sets quickly.
• This frosting colours beautifully
if you want a pastel-coloured cake
to fit in with the colour theme of
your event.
• The cakes can be frosted one
day ahead, however, the frosting
loses its sheen once it has set.
The flowers should be prepared
and placed on the day of serving.

Step 1 *Beat the fluffy frosting
in a small bowl with an electric
mixer until it is thick, spreadable
and almost cooled to room
temperature.*

Step 2 *Make sure you're ready to
spread the frosting onto the cake
as soon as it's ready; you need to
work quickly before the frosting
sets.*

Step 3 *On the day of serving,
trim flower stems to lie neatly on
top of the cake. Wrap stems in
florist's tape; position flowers on
top of cake.*

MERINGUE CLOUD CAKE

equipment
oven trays
medium offset metal spatula
large piping bag
7.5mm plain piping tube
30cm and 15cm round cake
    boards (page 137)
3 wooden skewers
craft glue

meringue
8 egg whites
440g caster sugar
2 tablespoons cornflour
2 teaspoons white vinegar

cake
deep 20cm and 15cm round
    cakes of choice (pages
    102–117)

decorations
300ml double cream
125g fresh raspberries
50cm wide ribbon

1 Preheat oven to 120°C. Line oven trays with baking parchment. Mark an 18cm circle on one tray; turn parchment over. Mark 9cm straight lines (you need about 100) on remaining trays; turn parchment over.
2 To make meringue, beat egg whites in large bowl with electric mixer to soft peaks; gradually add sugar, beat until dissolved between additions. Beat in sifted cornflour and vinegar. Using spatula, spread half the mixture inside circle on tray. Shape sides up and in towards centre (step 1).
3 Fit piping bag with tube. Half-fill bag with meringue; pipe 100 x 9cm finger-width meringue sticks, about 2cm apart, on remaining oven trays (step 2). Refill bag as necessary. Bake large meringue about 1 hour and the sticks about 30 minutes, or until dry to touch. Remove from oven; cool on trays.
4 Beat cream in small bowl with electric mixer until firm peaks form; cover, refrigerate until needed.

5 Trim cakes (page 120). Secure large cake to largest board; secure small cake to small board (page 120). Push trimmed skewers into large cake to support top tier (page 134). Secure small cake on top of large cake. Spread cakes all over with cream.
6 Position meringue sticks around sides of both cakes. Scoop out large spoonfuls of meringue; place between the tiers and on the top of small cake (step 3).
7 Sprinkle cake with raspberries. Wrap ribbon around large cake, secure ends with glue.

tips If short on oven space, halve the meringue recipe and make the large meringue and the sticks separately.
• The cake can be assembled and covered with cream one day ahead; store in the refrigerator.
• Arrange meringue sticks and spoonfuls of meringue as close to serving as possible. Meringues will soften in about 1 hour.

Step 1 Mark an 18cm circle on baking parchment, invert onto an oven tray. Spread meringue inside the circle, and shape inwards and upwards.

Step 2 Fit the piping bag with the tube. Pipe finger lengths of meringue, using markings as a guide, onto the baking-parchment-covered trays.

Step 3 Avoiding browned or caramelised meringue, scoop out large tablespoons of soft meringue onto top of cake and around top of large cake.

COCONUT RUFFLE CAKE

equipment
40cm, 30cm, 25cm, 20cm and 15cm round cake boards (page 137)
12 wooden skewers
medium offset metal spatula

cake
deep 35cm, 30cm, 25cm, 20cm and 15cm round cakes of choice (pages 102–117)

decorations
5 quantities white chocolate ganache (page 126)
white food colouring
1kg raw coconut chips

1 Trim cakes (page 120). Secure largest cake to largest board with a little ganache (page 120). Secure the remaining cakes to same-sized boards.
2 Push three trimmed skewers into centres of all cakes except the smallest cake to support the next tier (page 134).
3 Assemble cake, securing each tier to the tier below (page 135).
4 Place half the ganache in a large bowl; whisk in at least 1 tablespoon of white colouring until the ganache is as white as possible (*step 1*). Beat ganache with an electric mixer until light and fluffy (*step 2*). Repeat with remaining ganache.
5 Spread cake all over with ganache. Gently press handfuls of the flaked coconut all over the cake (*step 3*).

tips Coconut chips are available at health food shops and online.
• Instead of making the ganache you could buy five 453g tubs of vanilla frosting to cover this cake.
• This cake can be assembled completely a week before it's required; It will be fine kept in a cool place.
• Use any cake recipe you like – our favourite is the coconut cake (page 108).
• This five-tier cake is very heavy to move and lift, so get someone to help you.

Step 1 Place half the ganache in a large bowl. Whisk at least 1 tablespoon of food colouring into the ganache to whiten it as much as possible.

Step 2 Beat half the ganache at a time in large bowl with electric mixer until light and fluffy, scrape down side of bowl during beating.

Step 3 Once the cake is covered with the ganache, firmly press handfuls of coconut all over the cake. Choose long flakes for the top tier.

EXPERIENCED

HEAVENLY HYDRANGEA CUPCAKES

equipment
12 plain white paper cases
non-stick rolling pin
1.5cm 4-petal blossom cutter
vinyl mat
flower mat
small ball tool
4 paper piping bags (page 131)
fine artist's paint brush
5.5cm round cutter

cake
1 quantity cupcake mixture of
   choice (pages 102–117)

decorations
1.5kg ready-made white icing
cornflour
pink, violet and blue food
   colourings
1 quantity royal icing (page 121)
pink, green and violet petal dust
1 quantity ganache of choice
   (page 126)
12 fancy white paper wrappers

1 Divide cupcake mixture into paper cases; bake cupcakes according to recipe. Stand cakes in tin 5 minutes; turn top-side up onto wire rack to cool.

2 Knead ready-made icing on cornfloured surface until icing loses its stickiness. Divide into four portions. Tint three portions shades of blues, pinks and mauves; leave remaining portion white. Wrap each in cling film.
3 To make blossoms: Working with one colour at a time, roll small portions of icing on cornfloured surface into 3mm thickness. Using blossom cutter, cut five blossoms at a time; cover remaining icing with vinyl mat.
4 Place blossoms on flower mat; using small end of ball tool, roll tool in centre of each petal to round and thin the petals (*step 1*). Stand overnight on baking parchment to dry. Repeat with remaining icings. Re-roll scraps with remaining icing of same colour; reserve, covered with cling film.
5 Divide royal icing into four small bowls. Colour three portions to match colours of blossoms; leave remaining portion white. Cover with cling film to keep airtight.

6 Half-fill each piping bag with one coloured icing, pipe same-coloured dots into centres of blossoms (*step 2*); allow to dry overnight. Reserve all royal icing; cover surface to keep airtight.
7 Mix equal amounts of cornflour and petal dusts to complement blossom colours. Brush dust lightly into centres of blossoms.
8 Spread ganache over cupcakes. Roll out one of the reserved colours of ready-made icing on cornfloured surface into 3mm thickness. Use round cutter to cut out three rounds of icing, position over ganache (*step 3*). Place cakes in fancy wrappers. Repeat with the remaining colours.
9 Secure blossoms to same-coloured icing rounds on cupcakes to resemble hydrangeas using leftover royal icing.

makes 12
tips The blossoms can be completed months ahead. Keep in an airtight container at room temperature.
• Assemble cakes up to a day ahead.

Step 1 Cut out several blossoms at a time; place on flower mat. Use ball tool to shape and thin the petals; dry overnight.

Step 2 Pipe centres into blossoms with royal icing; leave to dry. Brush combined petal dust and cornflour over the centres.

Step 3 Spread tops of cupcakes with ganache. Top with rounds of ready-made icing to seal the cakes as much as possible.

AUTUMN LEAVES

equipment
35cm, 20cm and 15cm round
    cake boards (page 137)
non-stick rolling pin
smoothing tools
6 wooden skewers
paper piping bag (page 131)

cake
deep 25cm, 20cm and 15cm
    round cakes of choice (pages
    102–117)

decorations
1.4kg ready-made white icing
cornflour
orange and brown food
    colourings
1 quantity royal icing (page 121)
freshly picked organic leaves
    (see tips)
2m narrow ribbon

1 Trim cakes (page 120). Secure large cake to largest board; secure remaining cakes to the same-sized boards (page 120). Prepare cakes for covering with ready-made icing (page 120).
2 Knead ready-made icing on surface dusted with a little cornflour until icing loses its stickiness. Divide icing into three portions: 300g, 500g and 600g.
3 Use both colourings to tint all the icings three different autumnal shades. Colour the largest portion the darkest, the middle portion the palest and the smallest portion a medium shade.
4 Roll the largest portion of icing on cornfloured surface until large enough to cover largest cake. Using rolling pin, lift icing onto cake; smooth with hands then smoothing tools. Trim neatly around base of cake. Use medium portion of icing to cover medium cake in the same way. Use remaining icing to cover small cake. Dry cakes overnight.
5 Push three trimmed skewers into centres of large and medium

cakes to support the next tier (page 134).
6 Assemble cakes, securing each tier to the tier below (page 135).
7 Divide royal icing into three bowls; tint with colourings to match cakes. Half-fill piping bag with icing; pipe around base of same-coloured cake. Use fingertip to blend icing into any gaps where cakes join the boards (page 134). Dry cakes overnight.
8 Wash leaves carefully in cold water; leave to dry on absorbent paper (*step 1*).
9 Wrap and secure ribbon around base of each tier with a dot of royal icing (*step 2*). Pipe dots of icing onto backs of leaves; position leaves on cake (*step 3*).

tips We used leaves from a Japanese maple tree. If you choose different leaves, check they're organic and free from toxins. Wash, dry and position leaves as close to serving time as possible. Use small silk or dried leaves, if you prefer.

Step 1 Gently wash trimmed leaves in cold water; shake off excess water. Place the leaves on absorbent paper; leave until dry.

Step 2 Measure round each cake, cut ribbon into corresponding lengths. Position around cakes; join ends with a little royal icing.

Step 3 Position the leaves on the cake. Pipe tiny dots of royal icing onto the back of the leaves to secure to the cake.

CHERRY BLOSSOMS IN SPRING

equipment
30cm and 15cm round cake
    boards (page 137)
non-stick rolling pin
smoothing tools
3 wooden skewers
2 paper piping bags (page 131)
5-petal plunger cutter set (small,
    medium and large)
vinyl mat
ball tool
2 fine artist's paint brushes
tweezers

cake
2 x deep 20cm round cakes of
    choice (pages 102–117)
deep 15cm round cake of choice
    (pages 102–117)
shallow 15cm round cake of
    choice (pages 102–117)
jam or ganache of choice (page
    134)

decorations
1.5kg ready-made white icing
cornflour
rose pink, brown and black food
    colourings
1 quantity royal icing (page 121)
100g modelling paste
magenta petal dust
2 bunches small white stamens

1 Trim cakes (page 120). Secure one 20cm cake to largest board; top with remaining 20cm cake, joining cakes with a little jam or ganache (page 134). Secure deep 15cm cake to smaller board; top with remaining small cake, joining cakes with jam or ganache. Prepare cakes for covering with ready-made icing (page 120).
2 Knead ready-made icing on surface dusted with a little cornflour until icing loses its stickiness. Tint icing pink with colouring.
3 Roll one-third of the icing on cornfloured surface until large enough to cover small cake. Using rolling pin, lift icing onto cake; smooth with hands then smoothing tools. Trim icing neatly around base of cake; reserve scraps.
4 Use remaining icing to cover large cake the same way as small cake; reserve scraps. Dry cakes overnight.
5 Push trimmed skewers into centre of large cake to support the top tier. Secure small cake on top of large cake (page 135).
6 Reserve 1 heaped tablespoon of royal icing. Tint remaining royal icing pink to match cakes. Three-quarters fill piping bag with icing; pipe around base of each cake. Use fingertip to blend icing into any gaps where the cakes join the boards (page 135). Dry cakes overnight.

7 Knead modelling paste on surface dusted with cornflour until it loses its stickiness. Roll out a little of the paste to 1mm thick. Cut several blossoms from paste using all cutters (*see step 1 on page 48*). Cover the surface of the paste with the vinyl mat to prevent it from drying out.
8 Working quickly, place a blossom in palm of hand dusted with a little cornflour. Using small end of ball tool, gently press tool into blossom to round the petals and centre of blossom (*step 2*). Place blossoms on baking-parchment-lined tray to dry overnight. Repeat with more paste. You need about 35 small, 35 medium and 10 large blossoms.
9 Using paint brush, dust centre of blossoms with equal quantities of combined cornflour and petal dust (*step 3*).
10 Cut stamens to about 1cm long. Half-fill piping bag with reserved white royal icing; pipe a small dot of icing in centre of six blossoms. Use tweezers to position a few stamens in the icing in each blossom before it sets (*step 4*); stand until dry. Repeat with remaining blossoms.
11 Colour scraps of reserved ready-made icing brown using a little black and brown colouring.
12 Roll brown icing into thin strips of random thicknesses, lengths and shapes to resemble

cherry blossom branches (*step 5*); brush a little water on backs of branches, secure to cakes while still soft and pliable (*step 6*).

13 Secure blossoms to branches with a little royal icing.

tips Squeeze some of the icing strips for the branches with your fingertips to make them look gnarled and twisted. Secure the branches to the cake before they dry.

• Position all the branches first, followed by the blossoms. Flower blossoms can be made several weeks ahead. Store at room temperature in an airtight container.

Step 1 Using petal cutters, cut out a few different-sized blossoms at a time; keep them covered with the vinyl mat to prevent them drying out.

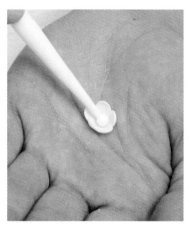

Step 2 Using the small end of the ball tool, shape blossoms by gently moving tool around the centres of the blossoms; dry overnight.

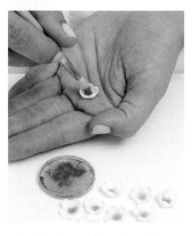

Step 3 Using a fine dry paint brush, dust centres of blossoms with equal quantities of combined cornflour and magenta-coloured petal dust.

Step 4 Pipe small dots of white royal icing into the centres of about six blossoms. Use tweezers to position several stamens before icing sets.

Step 5 Roll thin strips of brown icing into random lengths, thicknesses and shapes to make the branches for the cherry blossoms.

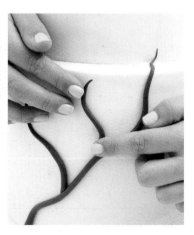

Step 6 While icing is still soft and pliable, position branches on the cakes in a random way; brush backs of branches with a little water to secure.

DIAMONDS ARE FOREVER

equipment
32cm and 18cm square cake
  boards (page 137)
non-stick rolling pin
smoothing tools
5cm x 8.5cm diamond patchwork
  cutter
4 wooden skewers
paper piping bag (page 131)
fine pearl-headed pin
tweezers
white florist's tape

cake
2 x deep 22cm square cakes of
  choice (pages 102–117)
deep 18cm square cake of choice
  (pages 102–117)
shallow 18cm square cake of
  choice (pages 102–117)
jam or ganache of choice
  (page 134)

decorations
1.6kg ready-made white icing
cornflour
1 quantity royal icing (page
  121)
2m narrow ribbon
72 x 3mm clear edible diamonds
fresh organic flowers

1 Trim cakes (page 120). Secure one 22cm cake to largest board; top with remaining 22cm cake, joining cakes with a little jam or ganache (page 134). Secure deep 18cm cake to smaller board; top with remaining small cake, joining cakes with jam or ganache. Prepare cakes for covering with ready-made icing (page 120).

2 Knead ready-made icing on surface dusted with a little cornflour until icing loses its stickiness.
3 Roll 700g of the icing on surface dusted with a little cornflour until large enough to cover small cake. Using rolling pin, lift icing onto cake; smooth with hands then smoothing tools. Trim icing neatly around base of cake.
4 Use remaining icing and scraps to cover the large cake in the same way.
5 While the icing is still soft, press diamond patchwork cutter all around cake to give quilted effect (step 1). Dry cakes overnight.
6 Push trimmed skewers into centre of large cake to support top tier. Secure small cake on large cake (page 135).
7 Three-quarters fill piping bag with royal icing; pipe around base of each cake. Use fingertip to blend icing into any gaps where

cakes join the boards (page 135). Dry cakes overnight.
8 Wrap ribbon around base of each cake; secure with a little royal icing.
9 Secure edible diamonds to joins in the pattern with a dab of royal icing (step 2).
10 Wrap stems of flowers with florist's tape; top cake with flowers.

tips Ask the florist to make you an appropriate arrangement for the top of the cake – they will tape the stems of the flowers for you. Prepare and place the flowers on the day of serving.
• The edible diamonds are not fragile to handle, but they do lose their sparkle quickly, so attach the diamonds to the cake as late as possible (up to 3 hours is ideal). Use tweezers or cotton gloves when handling the diamonds, as the natural oils in your fingertips can make the surface of the diamonds dull.

Step 1 While the icing is still soft, gently press the patchwork cutter into the icing all over the bottom cake.

Step 2 Working with one diamond at a time, pipe a dot of royal icing, then use the tweezers to carefully position diamond.

DIVINE WHITE SILK ROSE CAKE

equipment
30cm and 15cm round cake
  boards (page 137)
non-stick rolling pin
smoothing tools
number 3 strip cutter 7mm wide
3 wooden skewers
2 paper piping bags (page 131)
white florist's tape

cake
deep 20cm round cake of choice
  (pages 102–117)
deep 15cm round cake of choice
  (pages 102–117)
shallow 15cm round cake of
  choice (pages 102–117)
jam or ganache of choice (page
  134)

decorations
1kg ready-made white icing
cornflour
green food colouring
1 quantity royal icing (page 121)
1m wide ribbon
1m narrow ribbon
white silk cabbage rose or fresh
  organic flowers

1 Trim cakes (page 120). Secure large cake to largest board. Secure small deep cake to remaining board (page 120); top with shallow cake, joining with a little jam or ganache (page 134). Prepare cakes for covering with ready-made icing (pages 120).
2 Knead ready-made icing on surface dusted with a little cornflour until icing loses its stickiness. Tint half the icing pale green.
3 Roll icing on cornfloured surface until large enough to cover 20cm cake. Using rolling pin, lift icing onto cake; smooth with hands then smoothing tools. Trim icing neatly around base.
4 Use white icing to cover 15cm cake in the same way. While icing is still soft, use strip cutter to mark grooves into the icing on the top tier (*step 1*). Dry cakes overnight.
5 Push trimmed skewers into centre of large cake to support the top tier. Secure small cake on top of large cake (page 135).

6 Tint half the royal icing green to match the bottom tier. Three-quarters fill a piping bag with icing; pipe around base of cake. Use fingertip to blend icing into any gaps where cake joins the board (page 135). Repeat process using white royal icing for top tier. Dry cakes overnight.
7 Wrap ribbons around base of bottom cake; cut to fit. Secure ends with a little white royal icing (*step 2*).
8 Trim silk flower to fit top of cake (*step 3*). Wrap stem in white florist's tape. Gently prise open petals; lay flower on top of cake.

tips The strip cutter, used for marking the icing on the top tier of this cake, is very useful if the icing is not quite perfect.
• Position the flower on the day of serving.

![Step 1]

Step 1 Using the strip cutter, press it gently, but evenly, onto the soft icing before it begins to dry and develop a crust.

Step 2 Measure around the base of the bottom tier; cut ribbons to fit. Position and secure ribbons to cake with tiny dabs of royal icing.

Step 3 Trim the stem and leaves of the silk rose to fit the cake; tape stem with florist's tape. Gently prise open the flower petals.

21ST CELEBRATION CAKE

equipment
30cm and 15cm round cake
  boards (page 137)
non-stick rolling pin
smoothing tools
4 wooden skewers
2 paper piping bags (page 131)
number 1 and 2 cutters
2 x 10cm pieces 18-gauge floral
  wire
fine artist's paint brush
pasta machine
1cm plain piping tube

cake
deep 20cm and 15cm round
  cakes of choice (pages
  102–117)

decorations
1.5kg ready-made white icing
cornflour
pale blue, rose pink, yellow and
  orange food colourings
1 quantity royal icing (page 121)
3 teaspoons tylose powder

1 Trim cakes (page 120). Secure large cake to largest board; secure small cake to remaining board (page 120). Prepare cakes for covering with ready-made icing (page 120).
2 Knead 1kg of the ready-made icing on surface dusted with a little cornflour until icing loses its stickiness. Tint with blue colouring. Roll 400g of the blue icing on cornfloured surface until large enough to cover small cake. Using rolling pin, lift icing onto cake; smooth with hands then smoothing tools. Trim icing neatly around base. Use remaining icing to cover large cake in the same way. Dry cakes overnight. Reserve icing scraps, enclose in cling film.
3 Push three trimmed skewers into centre of large cake to support top tier. Secure small cake on top of large cake (page 135).
4 Tint royal icing blue to match cakes. Half-fill piping bag with royal icing; pipe around base of each cake. Use fingertip to blend icing into any gaps where cakes join the boards (page 135). Dry overnight. Cover the surface of the remaining royal icing with cling film to prevent it drying out.
5 Knead reserved icing scraps with three-quarters of the remaining white icing on cornfloured surface; tint icing to a darker blue colour.
6 Knead 1 teaspoon of the tylose powder into half of the dark blue icing; roll out to 6mm thickness on surface dusted with cornflour. Use cutters to cut out numbers (*see step 1 on page 57*). Dip one end of both pieces of wire about 2cm into water. Push wet end of wires into the bases of both numbers (*step 2*). Place numbers on baking-parchment-covered trays to dry overnight.
7 Roll remaining dark blue icing into 6mm-thick rope shapes (*step 3*). Brush lightly around base of cakes with a little water, gently position icing ropes around cakes. Carefully join ends.
8 Divide remaining white icing into four portions. Tint with pink, yellow and orange colourings. Leave remaining portion white. Cover with cling film.
9 To make strips: Knead ½ teaspoon tylose into one portion of icing. Roll out on cornfloured surface into 3mm thickness; roll through a pasta machine until 2mm thick (*step 4*). Cut 1cm x 10cm strips from icing. Coil strips around remaining skewer; carefully remove skewer (*step 5*). Use the tip of piping tube to cut dots from leftover scraps of icing (*step 6*). Stand strips and dots on baking-parchment-lined tray for about 30 minutes or until barely firm. Repeat with remaining icings.
10 Push wired numbers into cake. Three-quarters fill piping bag with royal icing. Decorate cake with 'confetti' and 'ribbons', securing to the cake with tiny dots of royal icing.

tip By using different colours and numbers, this cake would be suitable for a host of celebrations.

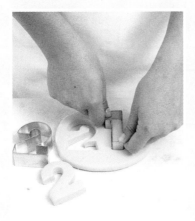

Step 1 Knead a teaspoon of tylose powder into one-third of the icing. Roll icing out on cornfloured surface to cut out numbers.

Step 2 Dip ends of both wires into water about 2cm. Push wet ends of wire about half way into the number shapes. Dry overnight.

Step 3 Roll icing into rope shape long enough to wrap around cakes. Brush a little water around cake bases and carefully position icing ropes.

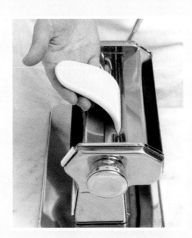

Step 4 To make decorations, feed icing through a pasta machine set on the thickest setting. Or roll out icing to about 2mm thickness.

Step 5 Coil strips of icing around a thick wooden skewer, place on baking-parchment-lined tray to dry for about 3 hours or overnight.

Step 6 Use tip of piping tube to cut out dots from different coloured icings. Dry for 3 hours or overnight on a baking-parchment-lined tray.

CHOCOLATE & IVORY HEARTS CAKE

equipment
non-stick rolling pin
7.5cm heart cutter
20cm 18-gauge floral wire
wire cutters
35cm, 20cm and 15cm round
    cake boards (page 137)
smoothing tools
6 wooden skewers
paper piping bag (page 131)

cake
deep 25cm, 20cm and 15cm
    round cakes of choice (pages
    102–117)

decorations
1.5kg ready-made ivory icing
cornflour
chocolate brown and ivory food
    colouring
1 quantity royal icing (page
    121)
5m narrow ribbon

1 Colour 40g ready-made icing
chocolate brown; knead on surface
dusted with a little cornflour until
icing loses its stickiness.

2 Roll icing out on cornfloured
surface into 3mm thickness. Using
cutter, cut a heart shape from icing
(*step 1*). Cut wire in half, push one
half into the heart shape (*step
2*); place on baking-parchment-
lined tray to dry overnight. Make
another heart in the same way
using 40g of the ready-made ivory
icing.
3 Trim cakes (page 120). Secure
large cake to largest board;
secure remaining cakes to same-
sized boards (page 120). Prepare
cakes for covering with ready-
made icing (page 120).
4 Knead remaining ivory icing on
surface dusted with a little cornflour
until icing loses its stickiness.
5 Roll 300g of icing on
cornfloured surface until large
enough to cover small cake.
Using rolling pin, lift icing onto
cake; smooth with hands then
smoothing tools. Trim icing
around base of cake.
6 Use 500g of the icing to cover
medium cake in the same way
as the small cake. Use remaining

icing to cover large cake in the
same way. Dry cakes overnight.
7 Push three trimmed skewers
into centres of large and medium
cakes to support the next tier;
assemble cakes, securing each
tier to the tier below (page 135).
8 Tint royal icing ivory to match
cake. Three-quarters fill piping
bag with royal icing; pipe around
base of each cake. Use fingertip
to blend icing into any gaps
where cakes join the boards
(page 135). Dry cakes overnight.
9 Cut ribbon in lengths long
enough to go around cakes.
Secure around cakes using tiny
dots of royal icing. Join ends of
ribbon with royal icing (*step 3*).
10 Position hearts on cake by
gently pushing wires into cake.

tips The hearts can be made
weeks ahead; store in an airtight
container. Position them on the
day of serving.
• It's best to secure the ribbon
after the icing has set completely,
which takes about 2 days.

Step 1 *Roll some of the brown
icing on a cornfloured surface.
Cut out heart shape. Repeat
using some of the ivory icing.*

Step 2 *Cut length of wire in half.
Push a piece of wire about halfway
into each heart. Dry on baking-
parchment-lined tray overnight.*

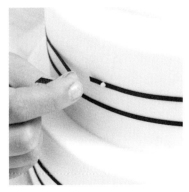

Step 3 *Measure and cut ribbons
to go around cakes. Secure
ribbons with tiny dots of royal
icing. Join ends with royal icing.*

LATTE LACE CAKE

equipment
40cm, 25cm, 20cm, 15cm and
  10cm square cake boards
  (page 137)
non-stick rolling pin
smoothing tools
16 wooden skewers
3 paper piping bags (page 131)
lace patterns (page 139)

cake
2 x deep 30cm square cakes of
  choice (pages 102–117)
deep 25cm, 20cm and 10cm
  square cakes of choice (pages
  102–117)
shallow 20cm, 15cm and 10cm
  square cakes of choice (pages
  102–117)
jam or ganache of choice (page
  134)

decorations
3.5kg ready-made ivory icing
cornflour
brown food colouring
1 quantity royal icing (page 121)
300g white chocolate Melts
1.5m wide ribbon

1 Trim cakes (page 120). Secure one 30cm cake to largest board (page 120); top with remaining 30cm cake, joining cakes with a little jam or ganache (page 134). Join the two 20cm cakes and the two 10cm cakes in the same way, securing cakes to same-sized boards (page 120). Secure 25cm and 15cm cakes to same-sized boards. Prepare cakes for covering with ready-made icing (page 120).
2 Knead 1kg ready-made icing on a cornfloured surface until icing loses its stickiness. Tint light brown with colouring.
3 Knead one-third of the icing on cornfloured surface. Roll icing until large enough to cover the 15cm cake. Using rolling pin, lift icing onto cake; smooth with hands then smoothing tools. Trim icing neatly around base of cake. Use remaining icing and scraps to cover the 25cm cake.
4 Knead remaining ivory icing on cornfloured surface; tint a darker shade than the previous cakes. Use 350g of the icing to cover

the 10cm cake; use 700g to cover the 20cm cake; use the remaining icing, plus scraps, to cover the 30cm cake. Dry cakes overnight.
5 Push four trimmed skewers into centre of all cakes except the top cake to support the next tier; assemble cakes, securing each tier to the tier below (page 134).
6 Tint royal icing to match the two colours of the cakes. Three-quarters fill two piping bags with each of the coloured royal icings; pipe around base of each cake to match the icing. Use fingertip to blend icing into any gaps where cakes join the boards (page 135). Dry cakes overnight.
7 Trace lace patterns (page 139) onto baking parchment; turn paper over (*step 1*). Melt chocolate (page 128). Half-fill piping bag with chocolate, snip tip off bag (*step 2*). Carefully pipe pattern onto paper; stand until set.
8 Pipe small dots of chocolate onto backs of chocolate lace (*step 3*); carefully secure lace to cake. Wrap ribbon around base of large cake; secure with royal icing.

Step 1 Carefully trace the lace patterns onto sheets of baking parchment; turn paper over so tracings are on the other side.

Step 2 Half-fill a paper piping bag with melted chocolate; pipe chocolate over patterns, then stand about 5 minutes or until set.

Step 3 Pipe dots of chocolate onto the back of one piece of lace; position on cake. Repeat to cover cake with lace pattern.

CHRISTMAS SNOWFLAKES

equipment
25cm round cake board (page 137)
non-stick rolling pin
smoothing tools
set of 3 snowflake plunger cutters (small, medium, large)
fine artist's paint brush
paper piping bag (page 131)

cake
deep 20cm round cake of choice (pages 102–117)

decorations
750g ready-made white icing
cornflour
cornflower blue food colouring
1 teaspoon tylose powder
1 egg white, lightly beaten
110g white sanding sugar
1 quantity royal icing (page 121)
180g sugared pistachios

1 Trim cake (page 120). Secure cake to board (page 120). Prepare for covering with ready-made icing (page 120).
2 Knead ready-made icing on surface dusted with a little cornflour until icing loses its stickiness. Tint three-quarters of the icing blue with colouring.
3 Roll out blue icing on cornfloured surface into 3mm thickness. Using rolling pin, lift icing over cake; smooth with hands then smoothing tools. Trim icing neatly around base of cake.
4 Knead remaining white ready-made icing with tylose powder on surface dusted with cornflour until smooth. Roll out on surface dusted with cornflour into 3mm thickness. Use cutters to cut out different-sized snowflakes. Place snowflakes on baking-parchment-lined tray to dry overnight.
5 Brush a very thin layer of egg white onto tips and around the centres of snowflake shapes (*step 1*); sprinkle sanding sugar over egg white. Stand the snowflakes for about 1 hour to dry (*step 2*).
6 Meanwhile, three-quarters fill piping bag with royal icing. Pipe a line of icing all the way around base of cake. Position persian confetti on icing before it dries.
7 Secure snowflakes to cake with royal icing (*step 3*); leave to dry for about 1 hour.

tips Sugared pistachios, also called persian confetti, are sold in speciality food stores and online. If you can't find any, then pipe snail's trail (page 132) around the base of the cake.
• Sanding sugar gives the snowflakes a lovely texture. If you can't find it, don't worry, the snowflakes look divine without it.
• Snowflakes can be made months ahead; store in an airtight container at room temperature.
• A fine dusting of sifted icing sugar added at the last minute adds to the snowy look.

Step 1 Using a fine artist's paint brush, brush a very thin layer of egg white onto the tips and around the centres of all the snowflakes.

Step 2 Sprinkle the centres and tips of the snowflakes with the sanding sugar; stand the snowflakes for about 1 hour or until they are dry.

Step 3 Pipe royal icing on the back of a snowflake, position on cake; hold large snowflakes for about 5 seconds until they grip the cake.

A POSY OF DAISIES

equipment
non-stick rolling pin
2.5cm and 1.5cm flower cutter
vinyl mat
flower mat
small ball tool
metal skewer
10cm polystyrene ball (available
    from craft shops)
1cm x 20cm wooden dowel
craft glue
small polystyrene block
30cm and 15cm round cake
    boards (page 137)
smoothing tools
3 wooden skewers
paper piping bag (page 131)
pastry brush

cake
deep 20cm and 15cm round
    cakes of choice (pages
    102–117)
1 quantity sugar syrup (page
    123)

decorations
150g modelling paste
cornflour
1m narrow ribbon
1kg ready-made white icing
lemon yellow food colouring
1 quantity royal icing (page 121)

1 Knead modelling paste on surface dusted with a little cornflour until paste loses its stickiness. Roll paste out on cornfloured surface into 1mm thickness. Using both cutters, cut out five flowers of each size at a time. Cover paste with vinyl mat to prevent it drying out.

2 Place five flowers on the flower mat; using the ball tool, press into the centre of each flower, in a circular motion, until the flower has thinned out and curled into a cup shape (*see step 1 on page 66*). Place the flowers on a fine wire rack or a baking-parchment-lined tray to dry. Repeat process until all the paste is used.

3 Push the metal skewer halfway into the polystyrene ball and wriggle it around to create a hole large enough to push the dowel into. Place a little glue around one end of the dowel, push dowel into hole in the ball (*step 2*). Stand 1 hour to dry. Spread a little glue along the back of the ribbon. Starting at the top of the dowel, wrap ribbon around the dowel (*step 3*). Allow to dry; stand ball upright in the polystyrene block to support it.

4 Trim cakes (page 120). Secure large cake to largest board; secure small cake to remaining board (page 120). Prepare cakes for covering with ready-made icing (page 120).

5 Knead ready-made icing on surface dusted with a little cornflour until icing loses its stickiness. Tint icing pale yellow.

6 Roll 300g of the icing on cornfloured surface until large enough to cover small cake. Using rolling pin, lift icing onto cake; smooth with hands then smoothing tools. Trim icing neatly around base.

7 Using 500g of the icing, cover large cake in the same way. Dry cakes overnight.

8 Push trimmed skewers into centre of large cake to support the top tier (page 134). Secure small cake to large cake (page 135).

9 Tint royal icing yellow to match cakes. Three-quarters fill piping bag with royal icing; pipe around base of each cake. Use fingertip to blend icing into any gaps where cakes join the boards (page 135). Dry overnight.

10 Pipe yellow centres into each of the flowers with royal icing (*step 4*); stand 3 hours or overnight to dry.

11 Brush polystyrene ball lightly with sugar syrup. Roll out remaining yellow icing until large enough to cover the ball. Using rolling pin, lift icing onto ball; smooth with hands then smoothing tools (*step 5*). Trim icing neatly around base of the ball.

12 Push dowel through the centre of the top cake until it reaches the board below. Using small and large flowers, pipe a dot of royal icing onto the back of a flower, position on the ball (*step 6*). Continue positioning flowers to cover the ball. Leave assembled cake to dry overnight.

13 Using picture as a guide, decorate both cakes with remaining flowers.

Step 1 Using the flower mat and the ball tool, shape flowers until a cup shape has formed and the petals become thinner.

Step 2 Using the large metal skewer, pierce the polystyrene ball. Wriggle it around to make a hole large enough for the dowel to fit snuggly.

Step 3 Glue dowel into ball; stand 1 hour to dry. Glue ribbon to dowel; wind it around dowel to the bottom, without completely covering.

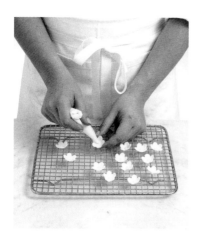

Step 4 Three-quarters fill a piping bag with yellow royal icing. Pipe dots in all the flower centres; leave flowers to dry overnight.

Step 5 Brush polystyrene ball lightly with sugar syrup. Gently mould icing over the ball, making it as neat as possible. Trim away excess icing.

Step 6 Pipe a dab of royal icing onto the back of a flower, position on polystyrene ball. Continue using large and small flowers to cover ball.

PINK ON WHITE FLOWER CAKE

equipment
35cm, 20cm and 15cm round
  cake boards (page 137)
non-stick rolling pin
smoothing tools
6 wooden skewers
fine long wooden skewer
silicone flower mould
small metal spatula
4 small piping bags
small (number 2) plain piping tube

cake
deep 25cm, 20cm and 15cm
  round cakes of choice (pages
  102–117)

decorations
2kg ready-made white icing
cornflour
tylose powder
rose pink food colouring
1 quantity royal icing (page 121)

1 Knead ready-made icing on lightly cornfloured surface until icing loses its stickiness. Reserve 200g of icing for flowers.
2 Trim cakes (page 120). Secure 25cm cake to largest board; secure remaining cakes to same-sized boards (page 120). Prepare cakes for covering with ready-made icing (page 120).
3 Roll 400g of the icing on surface dusted with cornflour until large enough to cover small cake. Using rolling pin, lift icing onto cake; smooth with hands then smoothing tools. Trim icing neatly around base of cake.
4 Use 600g of the icing to cover medium cake in the same way. Use remaining icing to cover large cake. Reserve icing scraps.
5 Use the fine wooden skewer to mark the icing in random lengths all around cakes before the icing sets (step 1). Dry cakes overnight.
6 Push three trimmed skewers into centres of large and medium cakes to support top tiers (page 134). Assemble cakes, securing each tier to the tier below (page 135).
7 Knead ½ teaspoon tylose powder into reserved icing and scraps. Divide into four portions; colour three portions different shades of pink. Leave remaining portion white. Press small amounts of each coloured icing into flower moulds; using spatula, scrape excess from backs of flowers so the shapes are flush with the mould. Bend mould gently to release flowers (step 2). Dry flowers, top-side up, on baking-parchment-lined tray overnight.
8 Fit piping bag with tube. Half-fill bag with royal icing. Pipe snail's trail (page 132) around base of each cake. Pipe white vertical lines in some of the grooves on the cakes. Wash and dry piping tube; place in clean piping bag.
9 Mix leftover icing in piping bag with remaining royal icing; divide between three small bowls. Colour each batch a different shade of pink; cover surface with cling film to keep airtight. Working with one colour at a time, pipe vertical lines in some of the grooves on the cakes. Repeat with remaining icings leaving some grooves plain (step 3). Wash and dry piping tube after each colour.
10 Using a few flowers at a time, pipe a little royal icing onto back of flowers; secure over cake in a random pattern.

Step 1 Using a fine wooden skewer, mark grooves of random lengths around the sides of all the cakes before the icing sets.

Step 2 Press small amounts of icing into mould, scraping away excess. Remove flowers from mould and allow to dry overnight.

Step 3 Pipe vertical lines of royal icing into the grooves using white and three shades of pink. Leave some grooves without icing.

EMBROIDERED BUTTON CAKE

equipment
45cm, 30cm, 25cm, 20cm, 15cm
and 10cm round cake boards
(page 137)
non-stick rolling pin
smoothing tools
15 wooden skewers
paper piping bag (page 131)
silicone button-shaped moulds
cooking-oil spray
small offset metal spatula

cake
deep 35cm, 30cm, 25cm, 20cm,
15cm and 10cm round cakes of
choice (pages 102–117)

decorations
5kg ready-made ivory icing
cornflour
1 quantity royal icing (page 121)
ivory food colouring

1 Trim cakes (page 120). Secure
35cm cake to largest board;
secure remaining cakes to the
same-sized boards (page 120).
Prepare cakes for covering with
ready-made icing (page 120).
2 Working with 2kg of the ready-
made icing, knead on surface
dusted with a little cornflour until
icing loses its stickiness. Roll 250g
of icing on cornfloured surface
until large enough to cover 10cm
cake. Using rolling pin, lift icing
onto cake; smooth with hands
then smoothing tools. Trim icing
neatly around base of cake;
reserve scraps.
3 Use 350g of icing to cover
15cm cake; 600g icing to cover
20cm cake and 800g icing to
cover 25cm cake in the same way
as step 2; reserve icing scraps.
4 Knead another 2kg icing with
scraps on cornfloured surface
until icing loses its stickiness. Roll
1kg on cornfloured surface to
cover 30cm cake; roll remaining
icing to cover 35cm cake in the
same way as step 2. Reserve icing
scraps. Dry cakes overnight.
5 Push three trimmed skewers
into centres of all cakes except
smallest to support the next tier;
assemble cakes, securing each
tier to the tier below (page 134).
6 Tint royal icing to match cakes.
Three-quarters fill piping bag with
royal icing; pipe around base of
each cake. Use fingertip to blend
icing into any gaps where cakes
join the boards (page 135). Dry
cakes overnight. Reserve royal
icing.
7 Knead remaining ready-made
icing with scraps on cornfloured
surface until icing loses its
stickiness. Lightly spray moulds
with cooking oil (*step 1*). Working
with a handful of icing, push small
amounts firmly into moulds (*step
2*). Use spatula to scrape excess
icing from backs of shapes so
icing is flush with the mould.
8 When mould is full, bend
slightly and lift out shapes; place,
flat-side down, onto baking-
parchment-lined trays to dry out
completely for 2 days.
9 Using a few buttons at a time,
pipe a little royal icing onto backs
of buttons; secure all over cake in
a random pattern (*step 3*).

tips You'll need to make around
400 buttons. This can be done
months ahead. Store shapes in an
airtight container.
• This cake looks most effective if
you use a wide variety of buttons
and flowers.

*Step 1 Spray surface of moulds
with cooking-oil spray. If the
shapes don't come out easily,
freeze for 2 minutes, then release.*

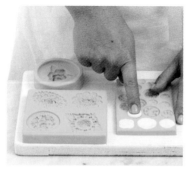

*Step 2 Working with a small
handful of icing at a time, push
enough icing into the lightly-oiled
moulds to tightly fill the shapes.*

*Step 3 Three-quarters fill a piping
bag with royal icing. Pipe dots of
icing on the backs of the buttons;
position randomly over cake.*

PETITE PINK CAKE

equipment
15cm round cake board (page 137)
non-stick rolling pin
smoothing tools
plastic ruler
pencil
fine pearl-headed pins
small piping bag
small (number 2) plain piping tube

cake
deep 15cm round cake of choice (pages 102–117)
shallow 15cm round cake of choice (pages 102–117)
jam or ganache of choice (page 134)

decorations
400g ready-made ivory icing
cornflour
1 quantity royal icing (page 121)
rose pink food colouring
fresh large organic flowers

1 Trim cakes (page 120). Secure deep cake to cake board with a little royal icing. Join shallow cake to deep cake with a little jam or ganache (page 134). Prepare cake for covering with ready-made icing (page 120).
2 Knead the ready-made icing on a surface dusted with a little cornflour until icing loses its stickiness, then roll icing on a cornfloured surface until large enough to cover the cake. Using rolling pin, lift icing onto cake; smooth with hands then smoothing tools. Trim icing

neatly around base. Stand cake overnight to dry.
3 Using picture as a guide, draw 'stitch' pattern onto a strip of baking parchment large enough to wrap around the cake; attach to cake, marked-side out, using pins. Using a fine pin, mark pattern onto the cake.
4 Tint royal icing pale pink. Fit piping bag with tube. Half-fill the bag with royal icing; pipe pattern onto cake using pin marks as a guide; leave to dry for at least 1 hour.
5 Position flowers on top of the cake on the day of serving.

tips Discuss the type of flowers to be used with a florist to make sure they'll stay fresh. Use artificial flowers, if you prefer.

Step 1 Measure around cake using a band of baking parchment; using pencil and ruler, draw 'stitch' markings of varying lengths onto the paper.

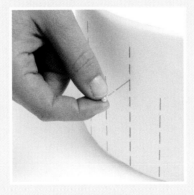

Step 2 Secure the band of baking parchment (marked-side outwards) around the cake with fine pins. Mark the pattern onto the cake with pins.

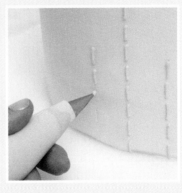

Step 3 Remove baking parchment. Fit piping bag with tube and, following the pin markings, pipe the pattern onto the cake. Leave to dry.

EXPERT

DUSKY ROSE CAKE

equipment
12 lengths 18-gauge floral wire
long-nosed pliers
flower glue (page 130)
polystyrene block
vinyl mat
3cm, 4cm, 5.5cm round cutters
flower mat
ball tool
fine artist's paint brush
small non-stick rolling pin
12-hole muffin tin or teacake
  mould
stamens
1.5cm 4-petal blossom cutter
florist's tape
45cm and 18cm round cake
  boards (page 137)
smoothing tools
3 wooden skewers
paper piping bag (page 131)

cake
deep 22cm and 18cm round
  cakes of choice (pages
  102–117)

decorations
2 quantities modelling paste
  (page 130)
rose pink and purple food
  colouring
cornflour
2kg ready-made white icing
1 quantity royal icing (page 121)

1 To make roses: Cut two lengths of wire into three 12cm lengths each. Make small hook at one end of each piece of wire using pliers (*see step 1 on page 77*).
2 Reserve 100g of modelling paste for blossoms. Colour one-third of the remaining paste dark pink, use to make six centres for four roses and two buds: Roll a marble-sized piece of paste into a rounded cone shape; dip hooked end of wire into flower glue, push halfway into broad end of cone (*step 2*). Push wire into polystyrene; dry overnight. Make five more centres in the same way.
3 When working with petals and blossoms, work with one at a time, and keep the remaining petals and blossoms covered with a vinyl mat.
4 Roll remaining dark pink paste on a cornfloured surface into 3mm thickness; using the 3cm cutter, cut out 3 petals, place on flower mat. Use ball tool to thin top of petal. Brush bottom third of petal lightly with flower glue; wrap around a bud (*step 3*). Secure and wrap remaining 2 petals around bud in the same way. Stand in polystyrene to dry overnight. Make 5 more buds in the same way. Reserve icing scraps.
5 Knead icing scraps into one-third of the remaining paste; use colouring to tint to a shade slightly lighter than the buds, if necessary. Roll paste on cornfloured surface until 3mm thick; cut out three 4cm petals (*step 4*).

6 Use rolling pin to thin top half of petal; place petal on flower mat, use ball tool to curl edge of petal. Secure around rose bud with flower glue. Repeat with the remaining two petals, overlapping each petal; dry overnight. Make five more buds in the same way.
7 Knead icing scraps into remaining paste; use colouring to tint to a paler shade than previous layer of petals.
8 To make the rose: Roll and cut out five petals using the 5.5cm cutter. Use rolling pin to thin top half of petals; place petals on flower mat, use ball tool to curl edge. Place petals in cornfloured muffin tin until edges of petals begin to firm. Glue in position around previous petals, overlapping each petal. Make three more roses the same way.
9 Make cup shapes from foil to support the outside petals. Place rose in foil cup, poke wire through foil. Suspend a wire cake rack above work top so the rose wire can sit in rack unimpeded while the rose is drying.
10 To make blossoms: Cut 10 pieces of wire into six equal lengths each. Cut 30 of the stamens in half. Roll half the reserved paste into a 3mm thickness; using 1.5cm cutter, cut out 30 blossoms (*step 5*).
11 Place five blossoms on flower mat (keep remainder under vinyl mat); shape petals with ball tool. Dab a dot of flower glue in centre of blossom; poke a

stamen through the glue (*step 6*). Repeat with remaining blossoms. Roll out remaining paste and make a further 30 blossoms. Dry blossoms overnight.

12 Gather five blossoms together, position a piece of wire close to the bottom of the blossom, secure stamens to wire with florist's tape (*step 7*).

13 Trim cakes (page 120). Secure large cake to large board; secure small cake to small board. Prepare for covering with ready-made icing (page 120).

14 Tint white ready-made icing mauve with purple colouring. Knead icing on cornfloured surface until icing loses its stickiness. Roll one-quarter of the icing on cornfloured surface until large enough to cover small cake. Use rolling pin to lift icing onto cake; smooth with hands then smoothing tools. Trim icing neatly around base; reserve scraps.

15 Use half the remaining icing to cover large cake in the same way as the small cake; dry cakes overnight.

16 Push trimmed skewers into centre of large cake to support top tier (page 134). Secure small cake on top of large cake (page 135).

17 Tint royal icing mauve to match cakes. Three-quarters fill piping bag with icing; pipe around base of each cake. Use fingertip to blend icing into any gaps where cakes join the board (page 135). Dry cakes overnight.

18 Knead reserved mauve icing and icing scraps on cornfloured surface. Roll icing large enough to make a 15cm x 30cm rectangle. Gently fold icing into three pleats (*step 8*). Gather and pinch ends together and, using picture as a guide, position and secure draped icing to cake with a little water (*step 9*); stand overnight to dry.

19 Position the roses and blossoms by gently pushing the wires into cake.

Step 1 *Cut 2 lengths of wire into three 12cm lengths. Using pliers, bend each piece of wire into a loop at one end to make a small hook.*

Step 2 *Roll a small piece of modelling paste into a cone shape. Dip hooked end of wire into flower glue, push into cone; dry overnight.*

Step 3 *For each rose, cut out three 3cm petals. Roll out the top half of each petal thinly, frill with a ball tool, then glue around the 'bud'.*

Step 4 *Cut out three 4cm petals for each rose, roll and frill the tops of each petal thinly. Position and secure on rose with flower glue.*

Step 5 *Using the blossom cutter, cut 30 blossoms from modelling paste. Place five blossoms on flower mat; shape using the ball tool.*

Step 6 *Dab a tiny dot of flower glue in the centre of a blossom; pull end of stamen through blossom to secure the tip on the glue.*

Step 7 *Gather five of the blossoms together, secure the stamens to a piece of wire by firmly wrapping with a single layer of florist's tape.*

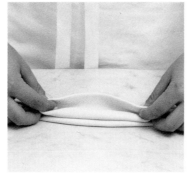

Step 8 *Roll mauve icing on a cornfloured surface into a 15cm x 30cm rectangle; gently fold the icing into three large pleats.*

Step 9 *Gently drape the icing over the cake. Gather the ends together and secure the ends of the icing to the cake with a little water.*

BRIDAL MOSAIC SQUARES

equipment
non-stick rolling pin
patchwork cutter trellis
star template (page 140)
fine pearl-headed pin
small piping bag
small (number 2) plain piping
  tube
paper piping bag (page 131)
small metal spatula
28cm square cake board (page
  137)

cake
deep 25cm square cake of choice
  (pages 102–117)

decorations
350g ready-made ivory icing
cornflour
1 quantity royal icing (page 121)
1 packet small pearlised blush
  sugar pearls (optional)
1 tablespoon strained lemon
  juice
1 quantity white chocolate
  ganache (page 126)

1 Knead ready-made icing on surface dusted with a little cornflour until icing loses its stickiness; roll out on surface dusted with cornflour into 3mm thickness. Cut nine 7.5cm squares from icing. Use the patchwork cutter to mark pattern on icing while icing is still soft. Place squares on baking-parchment-lined tray to dry overnight.
2 Cut around star template (page 139), place on top of dried icing square. Scratch outline into icing with a fine pin.
3 Fit piping bag with tube, half-fill bag with royal icing. Using picture as a guide, pipe patterns onto icing squares; pipe over patchwork outline (*steps 1–3*). Position pearls, if using, on royal icing before it dries. Stand overnight to dry.
4 For star shape, add a drop or two of lemon juice to the remaining royal icing – icing should be the consistency of

pouring cream. Spoon icing into paper piping bag; snip tip from bag. Pipe the icing inside the star points to 'flood' the star. Flood icing into any other shape as required. Stand overnight to set.
5 Trim cake top so it sits flat when turned upside down. Turn cake upside down, cut into 9 x 7.5cm squares.
6 Spread cakes evenly all over with ganache; freeze 10 minutes. Smooth ganache with a hot dry metal spatula.
7 Position cakes on board, top cakes with icing squares.

tips The icing squares can be made months ahead. Store them in a single layer (to protect the delicate piping) in airtight containers. Trim and cut the cakes a day ahead.
• The 'pearlized blush sugar pearls' are small edible pearls, and are available from cake decorating suppliers.

Step 1 Hold the piping bag at a 45-degree angle. Squeeze the bag firmly with an even pressure. Pipe a tiny dot of icing at the starting point.

Step 2 Continue to keep a firm pressure on the piping bag, lift the line of icing about 5mm from the surface of the icing square.

Step 3 Keeping the pressure even, touch down with the tip of the piping tube on the end of the icing square. Repeat to cover the square.

YELLOW PEONY ROSE CAKE

equipment
12cm length 18-gauge floral wire
long-nosed pliers
white florist's tape
non-stick rolling pin
pasta machine (see tips)
vinyl mat
small, medium, large and extra
    large peony cutters
wire cutters
7 lengths x 26-gauge floral wire
flower glue (page 130)
2 x 12-hole muffin tins or teacake
    moulds
peony petal veiner
flower mat
ball tool
fine artist's paint brush
35cm, 20cm and 15cm square
    cake boards (page 137)
smoothing tools
8 wooden skewers
3 paper piping bags (page 131)
craft glue

cake
deep 25cm, 20cm and 15cm
    square cakes of choice (pages
    102–117)

decorations
1 bundle small white stamens
100g modelling paste
ivory and lemon yellow food
    colouring
cornflour
yellow petal dust
2kg ready-made white icing
1 quantity royal icing (page 121)
4m wide ribbon

1 To make peony: Make a small hook in one end of the 18-gauge wire using pliers, don't fully close it (*see step 1 on page 83*). Fold the bunch of stamens in half, pull the centre of the stamens into the hook; close the hook by twisting the wire together with pliers (*step 2*). Secure stamens to wire with florist's tape (*step 3*).
2 Tint modelling paste ivory. Knead paste on surface dusted with a little cornflour until smooth. Roll paste on cornfloured surface until thin enough to be rolled through a pasta machine set on the thickest setting (see tips). Cover paste with vinyl mat.
3 Using petal cutters, cut three small, five medium, five large and seven extra large petals from paste (*step 4*); cover with vinyl mat.
4 Using wire cutters, cut each piece of 26-gauge wire into three even lengths. Work with one petal at a time, keeping remaining petals covered with vinyl mat. Thread one petal onto one piece of wire by dipping one end of wire into flower glue and gently pushing wire into pointed end of petal, one-third of the way into petal (*step 5*).
5 Dust muffin tins lightly with cornflour. Dust petal veiner with cornflour; press wired petal in petal veiner (*step 6*). Place petal onto flower mat; frill edge of petal by gently rolling ball tool over edge of petal (*step 7*). Place petal into muffin tin to dry overnight. Repeat with remaining petals.

6 To colour petals, combine a pinch of petal dust with a pinch of cornflour. Using paint brush, brush dust into centres of petals and stamens (*step 8*).
7 To assemble peony: Gently bend wire on a small petal to a 45-degree angle, hold against base of prepared flower centre (with stamens), secure by wrapping florist's tape once around wires (*step 9*). Repeat with remaining small petals, spacing evenly around centre of peony.
8 Continue wiring the petals in the same way using medium, then large, then extra large petals; placing each layer of petals evenly around flower centre slightly below the previous layer of petals.
9 Trim cakes (page 120). Secure 25cm cake to largest board; secure remaining cakes to same-sized boards (page 120). Prepare cakes for covering with ready-made icing (page 120).
10 Knead ready-made icing on cornfloured surface until icing loses its stickiness. Tint 500g icing very pale yellow, 700g a slightly darker yellow shade, and the remaining icing a darker shade again. Enclose, separately, in cling film.
11 Roll pale yellow icing on surface dusted with cornflour until large enough to cover small cake. Using rolling pin, lift icing onto cake; smooth with hands then smoothing tools. Trim icing neatly around base of cake.

12 Knead pale yellow icing scraps into medium-yellow icing; use to cover medium cake in the same way as small cake. Knead icing scraps into darkest yellow icing and use to cover the large cake in the same way. Dry cakes overnight.

13 Push four trimmed skewers into centres of large and medium cakes to support the next tier (page 134).

14 Assemble cakes, securing each tier to the tier below (page 135).

15 Divide royal icing into three bowls; tint each to match colour of the cakes. Half-fill piping bags to match cakes; pipe around bases of same-coloured cakes. Use fingertip to blend icing into any gaps where cakes join the boards (page 135). Dry overnight.

16 Trim ribbon to fit around bases of all tiers. Secure ends neatly with glue.

17 Gently push stem of peony into top of cake just before serving.

tips The petals can be made by rolling the icing out thinly to 2mm, rather than rolling through the pasta machine, however, the machine gives great results.
• A peony petal veiner and peony cutters are available from specialist cake decorating retailers.

Step 1 Using pliers, make a small hook on the end of the piece of 18-gauge wire. It should be barely large enough to hold the bunch of stamens.

Step 2 Fold the stamens in half and pull the centre of the stamens into the hook. Twist wire with pliers to hold the stamens securely in place.

Step 3 Firmly wrap the florist's tape around the stamens to secure them to the wire. Only wrap the base of the stamens to the wire.

Step 4 Roll the modelling paste through the pasta machine. Cut out three small, five medium, five large and seven extra large petals from the paste.

Step 5 Using a piece of 26-gauge wire, dip end of the wire into flower glue, push wire a third of the way into the pointed end of the petal.

Step 6 Dust the petal veiner with cornflour; working with one petal at a time, press the wired petal in petal veiner to create veins in icing.

Step 7 Place petal on the flower mat, frill the edge of the petal using the ball tool. Place petal in cornfloured muffin pan to dry overnight.

Step 8 Use equal amounts of combined petal dust and cornflour, and brush lightly onto petals, graduating the colour from dark to light.

Step 9 Bend wire on a small petal to 45 degrees, tape onto wire holding the stamens. Wire all petals in the same way, from small to extra large.

GIFT BOX FOR BABY

equipment
35cm square cake board (page 137)
non-stick rolling pin
smoothing tools
pasta machine (see tips)
1.4cm and 4.5cm perspex measures
vinyl mat
fine artist's paint brush
stitching tool
alphabet cutters
paper piping bag (page 131)

cake
2 x deep 20cm square cakes of choice (pages 102–117)
jam or ganache of choice (page 134)

decorations
2kg ready-made white icing
cornflour
pale green food colouring
1 quantity royal icing (page 121)
tylose powder

1 Trim cakes (page 120). Secure one cake to wooden board (page 120); top with remaining cake, joining cakes with a little jam or ganache (page 134). Prepare cake for covering with ready-made icing (page 120).

2 Knead ready-made icing on lightly cornfloured surface until icing loses its stickiness. Tint three-quarters of it pale green.

3 Roll 1kg of the green icing on cornfloured surface until large enough to cover cake. Using rolling pin, lift icing onto cake; smooth with hands then smoothing tools. Trim icing neatly around base of cake. Dry cake overnight. Knead green icing scraps into remaining green icing.

4 Using apricot-sized pieces of both the green and white icing, roll each out, separately, into a rectangle the width of the pasta machine. Feed pieces through the pasta machine set on the thickest setting (see tips) (*see step 1 on page 87*).

5 Using the 1.4cm perspex measure as a guide, cut 15cm lengths of green and white icing, each 1.4cm wide. You need 7 strips of each coloured icing for each side of the cake. Cover icing strips with vinyl mat to prevent drying out. Roll any icing scraps into same-coloured icing; cover, separately, with cling film.

6 Brush a little water onto the sides of the cake, secure icing strips to all sides of the cake, alternating colours (*step 2*).

7 Before the icing strips dry, Use 1.4cm perspex measure to mark sides of cake for lid. Dry cake overnight.

8 To make the lid: Brush a little water onto the area where the box lid will sit (*step 3*). Roll out remaining white icing on cornfloured surface until large enough to cover top of cake and extend over the sides to cover marked area for lid. Using rolling pin, lift icing onto cake; smooth with hands then smoothing tools. Use 1.4cm measure to mark the sides of the lid (*step 4*). Cut off excess icing with a sharp knife. Reserve icing scraps. Use stitching tool to mark pattern around bottom edge of lid. Dry cake overnight.

9 To make the plaque: Roll scraps of white icing on surface dusted with cornflour into 6cm x 16cm rectangle. Use stitching tool to mark edges. Roll half the remaining green icing into a 3mm thickness; use alphabet cutters to cut out letters (*step 5*). Outline letters with stitching tool. Half-fill piping bag with royal icing; secure letters to plaque with icing (*step 6*). Leave to dry overnight.

10 To make bow: Knead ¼ teaspoon tylose into remaining green icing. Roll out half the icing on surface dusted with cornflour into 3mm thickness. Using 4.5cm perspex measure, cut five strips of icing 4.5cm wide and 20cm long. Run stitching tool along both

edges of all strips. Fold strips in half to make loops, secure ends with a little water (*step 7*). Cut end into 'V' shapes, turn loops on their side on a baking-parchment-lined tray to dry overnight.

11 Roll out remaining green icing, cut four strips of icing 4.5cm x 20cm long. Run the stitching tool along both edges of all strips. Using picture as a guide, secure the icing strips to four sides of the cake with a little water (*step 8*). Roll scraps of icing long enough to make two tails for the bows; cut 'V' shapes into ends, secure to top of cake with a little royal icing. Position dried loops on cake to finish the bow; secure with royal icing (*step 9*).

tips The strips of icing can be made by rolling the icing out thinly to 2mm, however, rolling the icing through a pasta machine results in the icing being an even thickness all over.

• To make this cake look really good, it needs to look very square. Measure all the strips precisely.

Step 1 Set pasta machine to thickest setting. Roll a piece of icing into a rectangle the same width as the machine, feed through the machine.

Step 2 Cut strips of green and white icing long enough to cover each side of the cake. Secure alternate coloured strips to cake with water.

Step 3 Use a perspex measure to mark icing around the sides of the box where the lid will sit. Brush a little water over this area of the box.

Step 4 Roll icing out until it covers the top and sides of the cake. Use ruler to mark the sides of the lid. Cut off excess icing with a sharp knife.

Step 5 Make the plaque from scraps of white icing. Cut out letters from green icing. Use the stitching tool to mark the plaque and letters.

Step 6 Secure the letters to the plaque with a little royal icing. Stand the plaque on a baking-parchment-lined tray to dry overnight.

Step 7 Mark strips for bow with the stitching tool. Join ends of strips with water, trim ends into a 'V' shape. Turn loops on sides to dry.

Step 8 Roll strips of icing for the ribbon and tails for the bow, mark with stitching tool; position and secure to the cake with a little water.

Step 9 Half-fill a paper piping bag with royal icing. Pipe dots of icing onto the ribbon to secure the loops of the bow on the cake.

PRETTY PINK BOXES & BOWS

equipment
30cm, 15cm and 10cm square
   cake boards (page 137)
non-stick rolling pin
smoothing tools
2.5cm, 3cm and 3.5cm perspex
   measures
fine artist's paint brush
stitching tool
8 wooden skewers
3 paper piping bags (page 131)
vinyl mat
tape measure
cotton wool

cake
deep 20cm, 15cm and 10cm
   square cakes of choice (pages
   102–117)
shallow 20cm square cake of
   choice (pages 102–117)
jam or ganache of choice (page
   134)

decorations
3.3kg ready-made white icing
cornflour
rose pink food colouring
1 quantity royal icing (page 121)
tylose powder

1 Trim cakes (page 120). Secure deep 20cm cake to largest board (page 120); top with remaining 20cm cake, joining cakes with jam or ganache (page 134). Secure remaining cakes to same-sized boards. Prepare cakes for covering with ready-made icing (page 120).

2 Reserve 500g of the ready-made icing for bow. Knead 1.5kg of remaining icing on surface dusted with a little cornflour until icing loses its stickiness. Tint pale pink with colouring. Reserve 500g for box lid.

3 Roll remaining pale pink icing on cornfloured surface until large enough to cover largest cake. Using rolling pin, lift icing onto cake; smooth with hands then smoothing tools. Trim icing around base. Reserve icing scraps. Use 3.5cm perspex measure to mark sides of cake where lid will cover sides of box (*see step 1 on page 91*).

4 Tint 500g of the remaining white icing medium pink. Reserve 200g for box lid. Roll remaining medium pink icing on surface dusted with a little cornflour until large enough to cover small cake in the same way as the large cake. Reserve scraps. Use 2.5cm perspex measure to mark sides of cake for lid.

5 Tint remaining icing a darker pink. Reserve 300g for box lid. Roll remaining icing on cornfloured surface until large enough to cover medium cake in

the same way as the large cake. Reserve scraps. Use 3cm perspex measure to mark sides of cake for lid. Dry cakes overnight.

6 To make lids: Work with one cake at a time, using matching reserved icing and scraps, and corresponding perspex measure. Lightly brush a little water in marked area for lid (*step 2*). Roll icing out on cornfloured surface until large enough to cover top of cake and extend over sides to cover marked area. Use perspex measure and a sharp knife to cut away excess icing. Reserve scraps. Smooth icing with hands then smoothing tools (*step 3*).

7 Using the stitching tool, mark around the bottom edge of all the lids.

8 Push four trimmed skewers into centres of large and medium cakes to support the next tier (page 134). Assemble cakes, securing each tier to the tier below (page 135).

9 Divide royal icing into three bowls, tint to match cakes. Half-fill each of the piping bags with royal icing; pipe around base of same-coloured cake. Use fingertip to blend icing into any gaps where cakes join the boards (page 135). Dry cakes overnight.

10 To make ribbons: Take tiny pieces of the reserved icing scraps, roll into tiny balls (*step 4*). Place balls under vinyl mat. Knead two-thirds of the white icing on cornfloured surface until icing loses its stickiness.

11 Measure height of stacked cakes, roll out icing long enough to match height of cakes. Place dots randomly over icing; gently roll over the dots to push them into the icing (*step 5*). Cut a 3cm-wide rectangle of the required length. Secure ribbon to cakes with a little royal icing (*step 6*). Repeat process to make three more ribbons.

12 To make bow: Make more tiny pink balls, place under vinyl mat. Knead ½ teaspoon tylose into the remaining white icing on cornfloured surface. Roll icing on cornfloured surface until large enough to cut out a 10cm x 30cm strip and a 2.5cm x 20cm strip. Roll balls into icing the same way as the ribbon. Place large strip under vinyl mat. To make tails for bow, cut the small strip of icing in half crossways; cut 'V's into ends. Secure tails to cake with royal icing. Pinch the blunt ends of the tails to make narrower.

13 Cut the large strip of icing in half crossways. Place cotton wool on both rectangles of icing, fold icing over to enclose cotton wool, join edges with a little water (*step 7*). Gently pleat edges together (*step 8*). Stand each bow on one end almost touching; cover join with a scrap of icing, secure with a little water (*step 9*). Stand overnight to dry.

14 Remove cotton wool from bow when dry. Position bow on cake, secure with a little royal icing.

Step 1 Use perspex measure to measure sides of cakes for lids. Press the measure into the icing, to mark the area before the icing sets.

Step 2 Brush marked areas on sides of cakes with a little water. Cover cakes with reserved icing extending icing over sides; trim excess icing.

Step 3 Smooth the icing with the smoothing tools. Make the lids as square as possible, then use the stitching tool to mark pattern on lids.

Step 4 Using reserved scraps of all the icings, roll tiny balls of random sizes in palm of your hand. Keep the balls under the vinyl mat.

Step 5 Place the coloured icing balls randomly over the white icing. Gently roll over the balls with a rolling pin pressing the balls into the icing.

Step 6 Make the ribbons and tails for the bow; secure to cake stack with royal icing. Pinch blunt ends of tails to make them narrower.

Step 7 Cut the large strip of icing in half crossways. Position cotton wool on each rectangle; fold over icing, joining edges with water.

Step 8 Gently pinch and pleat joined edges of both rectangles to make the two halves of the bow narrow enough to join together.

Step 9 Push the halves of the bow together while standing the bow on its side. Cover the join with a scrap of icing. Push bow into shape.

BUCKLE UP BABY CAKES

equipment
non-stick rolling pin
5cm square cutter
buckle template (page 140)
4 paper piping bags (page 131)
16 plain yellow paper cases

cake
shallow 23cm square cake of
   choice (pages 102–117)

decorations
1kg ready-made white icing
cornflour
1 quantity royal icing (page 121)
lemon yellow food colouring
1 tablespoon strained lemon
   juice
2 egg whites
3m x 18mm wide ribbon

1 Knead a quarter of the ready-made icing on surface dusted with a little cornflour until icing loses its stickiness. Roll 200g of the icing on surface dusted with cornflour until 3mm thick. Using cutter, cut 16 x 5cm squares from icing. Transfer squares to baking-parchment-lined tray to dry. Reserve icing scraps.

2 Using buckle template (page 140), trace 16 buckles onto baking parchment. Turn paper over, place on a flat surface.

3 Tint half the royal icing yellow. Three-quarters fill piping bag with yellow icing; snip off tip. Pipe unbroken lines around the inner and outer edges of eight buckles (*see step 1 on page 94*). Spoon white royal icing into another piping bag, repeat to make eight white buckles. Allow to dry.

4 Add a drop or two of lemon juice to the remaining white royal icing – icing should be the consistency of pouring cream. Spoon icing into another paper piping bag; snip tip from bag. Using picture as a guide, pipe icing into the yellow buckles by piping into the space to flood the area (*step 2*). Repeat with the yellow royal icing and white buckles (*step 3*). Allow the buckles to dry overnight.

5 Trim cake into a 20cm square; cut cake into 16 x 5cm squares. Transfer cakes to wire rack; place rack over a tray. Secure icing squares to tops of all cakes with a little royal icing.

6 Chop half the remaining ready-made icing (including scraps) into medium heatproof bowl; add one lightly beaten egg white. Stir mixture over medium saucepan of simmering water (don't let water touch base of bowl). Gradually stir in about 1 tablespoon of warm water until the mixture becomes smooth and of a thick, slightly runny, (but not too runny) coating consistency. Do not over-heat the mixture.

7 Carefully pour the mixture over eight of the cake squares, covering the tops and sides of the cakes completely (*step 4*). Repeat process with remaining icing, egg white and water. Stand cakes about 1 hour or until the icing feels firm.

8 Cut ribbon into lengths long enough to extend over sides of each cake. Thread through the buckles (*step 5*). Place cakes into paper cases. Place a buckle on each cake, push the ribbon down the sides of the cakes. Push the paper cases against the icing on the cakes to form a seal (*step 6*).

makes 16
tips The squares of icing and the buckles can be made at least 2 weeks ahead.
• Make a few more buckles to allow for breakages.
• You could also secure the icing squares to the cakes using a little jam or lemon curd, if you prefer. The cakes can be completed up to 2 days ahead.

Step 1 Three-quarters fill a piping bag with royal icing. Pipe unbroken lines of icing around the inside and outside of the buckle shapes.

Step 2 Spoon the runny icing into a piping bag, snip the tip from the bag, and 'flood' the icing carefully into the centres of each buckle.

Step 3 Alternating the yellow and white royal icing, flood the runny icing into the outside areas of the buckles. Allow buckles to dry overnight.

Step 4 Heat ready-made icing gently with egg white and water until pourable. Stand cake squares on wire rack over tray; pour over icing.

Step 5 Cut ribbon into lengths long enough to extend over top and two sides of each cake. Carefully position ribbon through all the buckles.

Step 6 Position buckles on cakes, push end of ribbon onto sides of cakes. Press paper cases firmly onto icing on all sides of each cake to seal.

AFTERNOON TEA BISCUITS

equipment
non-stick rolling pin
oven trays
teacup cutter
teapot cutter
pastry brush
small piping bag
small (number 2) plain piping
  tube
1.4cm blossom cutter
2.5cm blossom cutter
tweezers

biscuits
125g butter, at room
  temperature
2 eggs, at room temperature
1 teaspoon vanilla extract
150g caster sugar
200g self-raising flour
150g plain flour

decorations
500g ready-made white icing
cornflour
mauve, rose pink, sky blue, leaf
  green and golden yellow food
  colourings
1 egg white, beaten lightly
1 quantity royal icing (page 121)
2 teaspoons pearlised sugar
  pearls

1 To make biscuits: Beat butter, extract and sugar in small bowl with electric mixer until combined. Beat in eggs, one at a time; beat only until combined. (Do not overbeat; mixture will curdle at this stage, but will come together later.) Transfer mixture to large bowl. Stir in sifted flours in two batches; mix to a soft dough. Knead dough on floured surface until smooth; cover, refrigerate 30 minutes.
2 Preheat oven to 180°C. Grease and line oven trays with baking parchment.
3 Roll dough between sheets of baking parchment until 5mm thick. Using teacup and teapot cutters, cut 10 of each shape from dough, re-rolling dough as necessary.
4 Place shapes, about 2.5cm apart, on trays. Bake about 15 minutes or until biscuits are firm and browned lightly. Stand biscuits on trays for 5 minutes; lift onto wire racks to cool.
5 Knead ready-made icing on surface dusted with a little cornflour until icing loses its stickiness. Divide icing into 5 equal portions. Tint each portion with one of the colourings; enclose, separately, in cling film.
6 Roll each icing portion, separately, on cornfloured surface until 3mm thick. Using cutters, cut 10 teacups and 10 teapots

from icings, re-rolling icing as necessary (*see step 1 on page 99*). Reserve all icing scraps, enclose, separately, in cling film.
7 Working with two or three shapes at a time, lightly brush tops of biscuits with egg white; position icing shapes on biscuits (*step 2*).
8 Fit piping bag with tube. Fill the bag three-quarters full with royal icing; pipe outlines and lines on biscuits, as pictured (*steps 3 and 4*).
9 Re-roll icing scraps on surface dusted with cornflour until 1mm thick; using blossom cutters, cut 20 small and 10 large blossoms from icing. Secure the 10 small blossoms to large blossoms with a little royal icing; secure to teapot biscuits (*step 5*). Secure remaining small blossoms to teacup biscuits with a little royal icing.
10 Pipe a dot of royal icing in the centre of each flower; using tweezers, position a pearl in flower centre (*step 6*). Pipe dots around flowers on teapots; pipe dots in teapot lids.

makes 20
tips You could use a paper piping bag without a tube to pipe the decorations on the biscuits.
• Pearlised sugar pearls are small edible pearls, and are available from cake decorating suppliers.

Step 1 Using both the teapot and teacup cutters, cut out shapes from the various coloured icings to match the number of biscuits.

Step 2 Working with two or three shapes at a time, brush biscuits lightly but evenly with egg white; position icing shapes on top of biscuits.

Step 3 Decorate the teacups by outlining their shape and handle with piped royal icing. Pipe vertical lines over teacup shape.

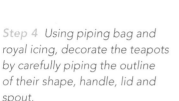

Step 4 Using piping bag and royal icing, decorate the teapots by carefully piping the outline of their shape, handle, lid and spout.

Step 5 Secure small blossoms to large blossoms with royal icing; secure to teapots. Pipe dots of icing around blossoms and in lid area.

Step 6 Pipe dots of royal icing in centres of about four flowers; position pearls on icing. Repeat with remaining flowers and pearls.

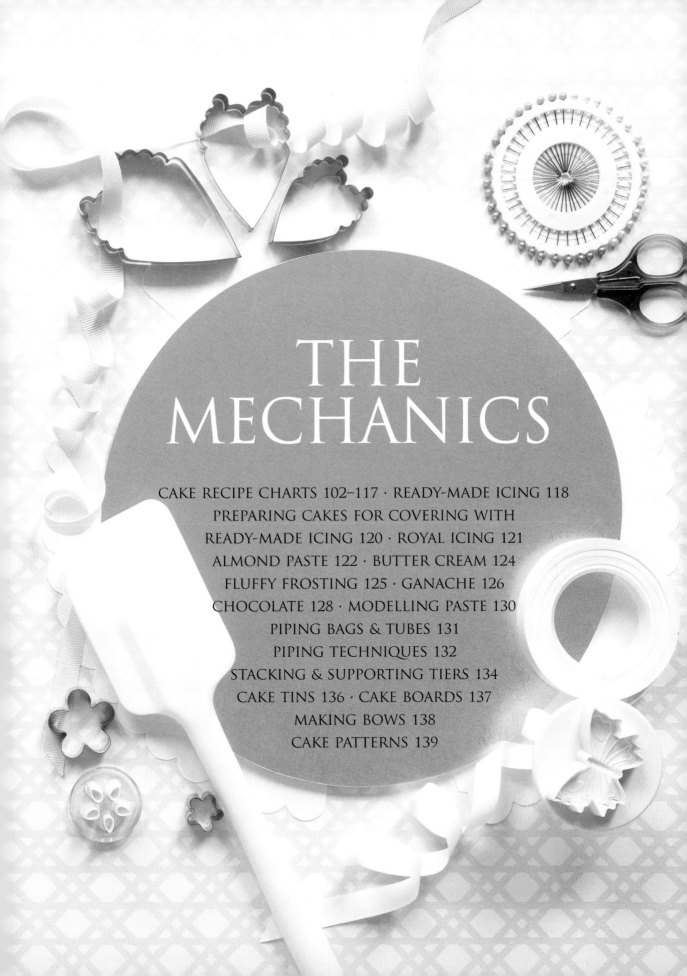

THE MECHANICS

BUTTER CAKE

Ingredients	deep 10cm round	deep 12cm round	shallow 15cm round	deep 15cm round	shallow 18cm round	deep 18cm round	shallow 20cm round
butter	50g	60g	60g	100g	100g	125g	125g
vanilla extract	¼ teaspoon	½ teaspoon	½ teaspoon	½ teaspoon	½ teaspoon	1 teaspoon	1 teaspoon
caster sugar	55g	75g	75g	110g	110g	165g	165g
eggs (60g)	1	1	1	1	1	2	2
self-raising flour	100g	110g	110g	185g	185g	225g	225g
milk	2 tablespoons	60ml	60ml	80ml	85ml	125ml	125ml
baking time (approx)	30 minutes	35 minutes	40 minutes	40 minutes	35 minutes	55 minutes	40 minutes

Ingredients	deep 20cm round	deep 22cm round	shallow 25cm round	deep 25cm round	deep 30cm round	deep 35cm round
butter	185g	250g	250g	375g	625g	740g
vanilla extract	1½ teaspoons	2 teaspoons	2 teaspoons	3 teaspoons	1 tablespoon	1½ tablespoons
caster sugar	220g	330g	330g	550g	825g	880g
eggs (60g)	3	4	4	6	10	12
self-raising flour	335g	450g	450g	675g	1.125kg	1.35kg
milk	185ml	250ml	250ml	375ml	625ml	750ml
baking time (approx)	1 hour	1¼ hours	45 minutes	1½ hours	1¾ hours	2 hours

Ingredients	shallow 10cm square	deep 10cm square	shallow 15cm square	deep 15cm square	shallow 18cm square	deep 18cm square	shallow 20cm square
butter	60g	65g	100g	125g	125g	185g	185g
vanilla extract	½ teaspoon	½ teaspoon	½ teaspoon	1 teaspoon	1 teaspoon	1½ teaspoons	1½ teaspoons
caster sugar	75g	75g	110g	165g	165g	220g	220g
eggs (60g)	1	1	1	2	2	3	3
self-raising flour	110g	110g	185g	225g	225g	335g	335g
milk	60ml	60ml	85ml	125ml	125ml	185ml	185ml
baking time (approx)	30 minutes	30 minutes	45 minutes	55 minutes	45 minutes	1 hour	45 minutes

Ingredients	deep 20cm square	shallow 22cm square	deep 22cm square	shallow 25cm square	deep 25cm square	deep 30cm square
butter	250g	250g	375g	375g	625g	740g
vanilla extract	2 teaspoons	2 teaspoons	3 teaspoons	3 teaspoons	1 tablespoon	1½ tablespoons
caster sugar	330g	330g	550g	550g	825g	880g
eggs (60g)	4	4	6	6	10	12
self-raising flour	450g	450g	675g	675g	1.125kg	1.35kg
milk	250ml	250ml	375ml	375ml	625ml	750ml
baking time (approx)	1¼ hours	1 hour	1½ hours	1¼ hours	1¾ hours	2 hours

Ingredients	deep 18cm heart shaped	deep 15cm octagonal	deep 20cm octagonal	12-hole muffin tin (80ml)
butter	125g	125g	250g	185g
vanilla extract	1 teaspoon	1 teaspoon	2 teaspoons	1½ teaspoons
caster sugar	165g	165g	330g	220g
eggs (60g)	2	2	4	3
self-raising flour	225g	225g	450g	335g
milk	125ml	125ml	250ml	185ml
baking time (approx)	1 hour	1 hour	1¼ hours	20 minutes

tips We used 7.5cm deep cake tins with straight sides.
• Butter, eggs and milk should be at room temperature for best results.
• The cake will keep well for 2 days in an airtight container, or can be frozen for 3 months.

1 Preheat oven to 180°C. Grease and line base and side(s) of cake tin with baking parchment, extending paper 5cm above side(s).
2 Beat butter, extract and sugar in bowl with electric mixer until light and fluffy. Beat in eggs, one at a time. Transfer mixture to larger bowl; stir in sifted flour and milk, in two batches. Spread mixture into tin.
3 Bake cake for the time given in chart. Cover cake with foil halfway through baking if cake is over-browning, or lower the oven temperature by 10–20 degrees if cake is over 20cm.
4 Test cake by inserting a skewer into centre of cake; if cooked, skewer will be clean, if there is cake mixture on the skewer, bake cake a further 10 minutes before testing again.
5 Stand cake in the tin for 10–30 minutes, depending on the size of cake, before turning, top-side down, onto wire rack to cool.

RASPBERRY HAZELNUT CAKE

Ingredients	deep 10cm round	deep 12cm round	shallow 15cm round	deep 15cm round	shallow 18cm round	deep 18cm round	shallow 20cm round
butter	55g	80g	80g	110g	110g	165g	165g
caster sugar	110g	165g	165g	220g	220g	275g	275g
eggs (60g)	1	2	2	3	3	4	4
plain flour	35g	50g	50g	75g	75g	110g	110g
self-raising flour	1½ tablespoons	2 tablespoons	2 tablespoons	35g	35g	50g	50g
ground hazelnuts	25g	35g	35g	50g	50g	75g	75g
soured cream	2 tablespoons	60ml	60ml	85ml	85ml	125ml	125ml
fresh or frozen raspberries	65g	100g	100g	130g	130g	190g	190g
baking time (approx)	50 minutes	1¼ hours	1 hour	1¼ hours	1 hour	1½ hours	1¼ hours

Ingredients	deep 20cm round	deep 22cm round	shallow 25cm round	deep 25cm round	deep 30cm round	deep 35cm round
butter	220g	275g	275g	385g	550g	880g
caster sugar	385g	440g	440g	660g	990g	1.54kg
eggs (60g)	5	6	6	9	13	20
plain flour	150g	185g	185g	260g	375g	600g
self-raising flour	75g	100g	100g	110g	185g	300g
ground hazelnuts	100g	125g	125g	175g	250g	400g
soured cream	165ml	185ml	185ml	250ml	415ml	665ml
fresh or frozen raspberries	260g	325g	325g	450g	650g	1kg
baking time (approx)	1¾ hours	2 hours	1½ hours	2½ hours	3 hours	3½ hours

Ingredients	shallow 10cm square	deep 10cm square	shallow 15cm square	deep 15cm square	shallow 18cm square	deep 18cm square	shallow 20cm square
butter	55g	80g	110g	165g	165g	220g	220g
caster sugar	110g	165g	220g	275g	275g	385g	385g
eggs (60g)	1	2	3	4	4	5	5
plain flour	35g	50g	75g	110g	110g	150g	150g
self-raising flour	1½ tablespoons	2 tablespoons	35g	50g	50g	75g	75g
ground hazelnuts	25g	35g	50g	75g	75g	100g	100g
soured cream	2 tablespoons	60ml	85ml	125ml	125ml	165ml	165ml
fresh or frozen raspberries	65g	100g	130g	190g	190g	260g	260g
baking time (approx)	45 minutes	1 hour	1¼ hours	1½ hours	1 hour	1¾ hours	1¼ hours

Ingredients	deep 20cm square	shallow 22cm square	deep 22cm square	shallow 25cm square	deep 25cm square	deep 30cm square
butter	275g	275g	385g	385g	550g	880g
caster sugar	440g	440g	660g	660g	990g	1.54kg
eggs (60g)	6	6	9	9	13	20
plain flour	185g	185g	260g	260g	375g	600g
self-raising flour	100g	100g	110g	110g	185g	300g
ground hazelnuts	125g	125g	175g	175g	250g	400g
soured cream	185ml	185ml	250ml	250ml	415ml	665ml
fresh or frozen raspberries	325g	325g	450g	450g	650g	1kg
baking time (approx)	2 hours	1¾ hours	2½ hours	2¼ hours	3 hours	3½ hours

Ingredients	deep 18cm heart shaped	deep 15cm octagonal	deep 20cm octagonal	12-hole muffin tin (80ml)
butter	165g	165g	275g	220g
caster sugar	275g	275g	440g	385g
eggs (60g)	4	4	6	5
plain flour	110g	110g	185g	150g
self-raising flour	50g	50g	100g	75g
ground hazelnuts	75g	75g	125g	50g
soured cream	125ml	125ml	185ml	165ml
fresh or frozen raspberries	190g	190g	325g	260g
baking time (approx)	1½ hours	1½ hours	2 hours	35 minutes

tips We used 7.5cm deep cake tins with straight sides.
• Butter, eggs and soured cream should be at room temperature for best results.
• If using frozen berries do not thaw them; frozen berries are less likely to 'bleed' into the cake mixture.
• The cake will keep well for 3 days in an airtight container, or can be frozen for 3 months.

1 Preheat oven to 160°C. Grease and line base and side(s) of cake tin with baking parchment, extending paper 5cm above side(s).
2 Beat butter and sugar in bowl with electric mixer until light and fluffy. Beat in eggs, one at a time. (Mixture will curdle at this stage but will come together later.)
3 Transfer mixture to a larger bowl; stir in the sifted flours and ground hazelnuts, soured cream and berries. Spread mixture into tin.
4 Bake cake for the time given in chart. Cover cake with foil halfway through baking if cake is over-browning, or lower the oven temperature by 10–20 degrees if cake is over 20cm.
5 Test cake by inserting a skewer into centre of cake; if cooked, skewer will be clean, if there is cake mixture on the skewer, bake cake a further 10 minutes before testing again.
6 Stand cake in the tin for 10–30 minutes, depending on the size of the cake, before turning, top-side down, onto wire rack to cool.

POPPY SEED & ORANGE CAKE

Ingredients	deep 10cm round	deep 12cm round	shallow 15cm round	deep 15cm round	shallow 18cm round	deep 18cm round	shallow 20cm round
poppy seeds	2 tablespoons	40g	40g	55g	55g	80g	80g
milk	3 teaspoons	1 tablespoon	1 tablespoon	1½ tablespoons	1½ tablespoons	2 tablespoons	2 tablespoons
butter	45g	70g	70g	100g	100g	140g	140g
grated orange rind	1½ teaspoons	2 teaspoons	2 teaspoons	3 teaspoons	3 teaspoons	1 tablespoon	1 tablespoon
caster sugar	55g	75g	75g	110g	110g	165g	165g
eggs (60g)	1	2	2	2	2	3	3
self-raising flour	75g	100g	100g	150g	150g	185g	185g
plain flour	1½ tablespoons	2 tablespoons	2 tablespoons	35g	35g	50g	50g
ground almonds	1½ tablespoons	2 tablespoons	2 tablespoons	25g	25g	35g	35g
orange juice	1½ tablespoons	2 tablespoons	2 tablespoons	60ml	60ml	85ml	85ml
baking time (approx)	30 minutes	45 minutes	40 minutes	50 minutes	40 minutes	1 hour	45 minutes

Ingredients	deep 20cm round	deep 22cm round	shallow 25cm round	deep 25cm round	deep 30cm round	deep 35cm round
poppy seeds	120g	160g	160g	160g	280g	320g
milk	2½ tablespoons	85ml	85ml	85ml	125ml	250ml
butter	175g	285g	285g	300g	370g	740g
grated orange rind	1 tablespoon	1½ tablespoons	1½ tablespoons	25g	30g	30g
caster sugar	220g	295g	295g	370g	440g	880g
eggs (60g)	4	4	4	5	6	12
self-raising flour	200g	225g	225g	550g	450g	900g
plain flour	75g	100g	100g	110g	150g	300g
ground almonds	60g	80g	80g	90g	120g	240g
orange juice	125ml	165ml	165ml	185ml	250ml	500ml
baking time (approx)	1 hour	1¼ hours	1 hour	1¼ hours	1½ hours	1¾ hours

Ingredients	shallow 10cm square	deep 10cm square	shallow 15cm square	deep 15cm square	shallow 18cm square	deep 18cm square	shallow 20cm square
poppy seeds	2 tablespoons	40g	55g	80g	80g	120g	120g
milk	3 teaspoons	1 tablespoon	1½ tablespoons	2 tablespoons	2 tablespoons	2½ tablespoons	2½ tablespoons
butter	45g	70g	100g	140g	140g	175g	175g
grated orange rind	1½ teaspoons	2 teaspoons	3 teaspoons	1 tablespoon	1 tablespoon	1 tablespoon	1 tablespoon
caster sugar	55g	75g	110g	165g	165g	220g	220g
eggs (60g)	1	2	2	3	3	4	4
self-raising flour	75g	100g	150g	185g	185g	200g	200g
plain flour	1½ tablespoons	2 tablespoons	35g	50g	50g	75g	75g
ground almonds	1½ tablespoons	2 tablespoons	30g	40g	40g	60g	60g
orange juice	1½ tablespoons	2 tablespoons	60ml	85ml	85ml	125ml	125ml
baking time (approx)	35 minutes	45 minutes	45 minutes	50 minutes	45 minutes	1 hour	45 minutes

Ingredients	deep 20cm square	shallow 22cm square	deep 22cm square	shallow 25cm square	deep 25cm square	deep 30cm square
poppy seeds	160g	160g	160g	160g	215g	320g
milk	85ml	85ml	125ml	125ml	125ml	250ml
butter	285g	285g	325g	325g	370g	740g
grated orange rind	1½ tablespoons	1½ tablespoons	2 tablespoons	2 tablespoons	25g	30g
caster sugar	295g	295g	385g	385g	440g	880g
eggs (60g)	4	4	6	6	6	12
self-raising flour	225g	225g	410g	410g	450g	900g
plain flour	100g	100g	150g	150g	150g	300g
ground almonds	80g	80g	120g	120g	120g	240g
orange juice	165ml	165ml	250ml	250ml	250ml	500ml
baking time (approx)	1¼ hours	1 hour	1¼ hours	1¼ hours	1½ hours	1¾ hours

Ingredients	deep 18cm heart shaped	deep 15cm octagonal	deep 20cm octagonal	12-hole muffin tin (80ml)
poppy seeds	80g	80g	120g	120g
milk	2 tablespoons	2 tablespoons	2½ tablespoons	2½ tablespoons
butter	140g	140g	175g	175g
orange rind	1 tablespoon	1 tablespoon	1 tablespoon	1 tablespoon
caster sugar	165	165g	220g	220g
eggs (60g)	3	3	4	4
self-raising flour	185g	185g	200g	200g
plain flour	50g	50g	75g	75g
ground almonds	40g	40g	60g	60g
orange juice	85ml	85ml	125ml	125ml
baking time (approx)	45 minutes	45 minutes	1 hour	25 minutes

tips We used 7.5cm deep cake tins with straight sides.
• Butter and eggs should be at room temperature for best results.
• The orange rind should be finely grated.
• The cake will keep well for 2 days in an airtight container, or can be frozen for 3 months.

1 Preheat oven to 180°C. Grease and line base and side(s) of cake tin with baking parchment, extending paper 5cm above side(s).
2 Combine seeds and milk in a small bowl, stand 20 minutes.
3 Meanwhile, beat butter, rind and sugar in a bowl with an electric mixer until light and fluffy. Beat in eggs, one at a time, until just combined between additions.
4 Transfer mixture to a larger bowl. Stir in the sifted flours, ground almonds, juice and the poppy seed mixture. Spread mixture into tin.
5 Bake cake for the time given in chart. Cover cake with foil halfway through baking if cake is over-browning, or lower the oven temperature by 10–20 degrees if cake is over 20cm.
6 Test cake by inserting a skewer into centre of cake; if cooked, skewer will be clean, if there is cake mixture on the skewer, bake cake a further 10 minutes before testing again.
7 Stand cake in the tin for 10–30 minutes, depending on the size of the cake, before turning, top-side down, onto wire rack to cool.

COCONUT CAKE

Ingredients	deep 10cm round	deep 12cm round	shallow 15cm round	deep 15cm round	shallow 18cm round	deep 18cm round	shallow 20cm round
butter	60g	90g	90g	125g	125g	185g	185g
coconut essence	½ teaspoon	¾ teaspoon	¾ teaspoon	1 teaspoon	1 teaspoon	1½ teaspoons	1½ teaspoons
caster sugar	110g	165g	165g	220g	220g	330g	330g
coconut cream	85ml	125ml	125ml	185ml	185ml	250ml	250ml
self-raising flour	75g	110g	110g	150g	150g	225g	225g
egg whites	2	2	2	3	3	4	4
baking time (approx)	50 minutes	1¼ hours	50 minutes	1¼ hours	1 hour	1¼ hours	1 hour

Ingredients	deep 20cm round	deep 22cm round	shallow 25cm round	deep 25cm round	deep 30cm round	deep 35cm round
butter	250g	310g	310g	500g	750g	1kg
coconut essence	2 teaspoons	2½ teaspoons	2½ teaspoons	3 teaspoons	1 tablespoon	1 tablespoon
caster sugar	440g	550g	550g	880g	1.32kg	1.76kg
coconut cream	375ml	435ml	435ml	750ml	1.125 litres	1.5 litres
self-raising flour	335g	450g	450g	675g	1kg	1.35kg
egg whites	6	7	7	12	18	24
baking time (approx)	1½ hours	1¾ hours	1¼ hours	2¼ hours	2½ hours	3 hours

Ingredients	shallow 10cm square	deep 10cm square	shallow 15cm square	deep 15cm square	shallow 18cm square	deep 18cm square	shallow 20cm square
butter	60g	90g	80g	185g	185g	250g	250g
coconut essence	½ teaspoon	¾ teaspoon	½ teaspoon	1½ teaspoons	1½ teaspoons	2 teaspoons	2 teaspoons
caster sugar	110g	165g	150g	330g	330g	440g	440g
coconut cream	85ml	125ml	125ml	250ml	250ml	375ml	375ml
self-raising flour	75g	110g	110g	225g	225g	335g	335g
egg whites	2	2	2	4	4	6	6
baking time (approx)	40 minutes	1 hour	1¼ hours	1¼ hours	1 hour	1½ hours	1½ hours

Ingredients	deep 20cm square	shallow 22cm square	deep 22cm square	shallow 25cm square	deep 25cm square	deep 30cm square
butter	310g	310g	500g	500g	750g	1kg
coconut essence	2½ teaspoons	2½ teaspoons	3 teaspoons	3 teaspoons	1 tablespoon	1 tablespoon
caster sugar	550g	550g	880g	880g	1.32kg	1.76kg
coconut cream	435ml	435ml	750ml	750ml	1.125 litres	1.5 litres
self-raising flour	450g	450g	675g	675g	1kg	1.35kg
egg whites	7	7	12	12	18	24
baking time (approx)	1½ hours	1 hour	2¼ hours	1¾ hours	2½ hours	3 hours

Ingredients	deep 18cm heart shaped	deep 15cm octagonal	deep 20cm octagonal	12-hole muffin tin (80ml)
butter	185g	185g	310g	250g
coconut essence	1½ teaspoons	1½ teaspoons	2½ teaspoons	2 teaspoons
caster sugar	330g	330g	550g	440g
coconut cream	250ml	250ml	435ml	375ml
self-raising flour	225g	225g	450g	335g
egg whites	4	4	7	6
baking time (approx)	1½ hours	1½ hours	1¾ hours	45 minutes

tips We used 7.5cm deep cake tins with straight sides.
• Butter and egg whites should be at room temperature for best results.
• We used canned coconut cream.
• This cake is quite soft, and needs to be cooled in the tin before turning out. The cake will keep well for 3 days in an airtight container, or it can be frozen for 3 months.

1 Preheat oven to 160°C. Grease and line base and side(s) of cake tin with baking parchment, extending paper 5cm above side(s).
2 Beat butter, essence and sugar in bowl with electric mixer until light and fluffy. Transfer mixture to a larger bowl; stir in coconut cream and sifted flour, in two batches.
3 Beat egg whites in bowl with electric mixer until soft peaks form. The egg whites need to be beaten in a narrow bowl so that the beaters are well down in the egg whites to create the necessary volume. Fold egg whites into coconut mixture, in two batches. Spread mixture into tin.
4 Bake cake for the time given in chart. Cover cake with foil halfway through baking if cake is over-browning, or lower the oven temperature by 10–20 degrees if cake is over 20cm.
5 Test cake by inserting a skewer into centre of cake; if cooked, skewer will be clean, if there is cake mixture on the skewer, bake cake a further 10 minutes before testing again. Cool cake in tin.

CARROT CAKE

Ingredients	deep 10cm round	deep 12cm round	shallow 15cm round	deep 15cm round	shallow 18cm round	deep 18cm round	shallow 20cm round
self-raising flour	35g	50g	50g	75g	75g	110g	150g
plain flour	2 tablespoons	35g	35g	50g	50g	75g	75g
bicarb. of soda	¼ teaspoon	¼ teaspoon	¼ teaspoon	½ teaspoon	½ teaspoon	½ teaspoon	½ teaspoon
mixed spice	½ teaspoon	1 teaspoon	1 teaspoon	1 teaspoon	1 teaspoon	2 teaspoons	2 teaspoons
light brown sugar	2 tablespoons	55g	55g	75g	75g	110g	110g
coarsely grated carrot	120g	180g	180g	240g	240g	360g	360g
vegetable oil	1½ tablespoons	60ml	60ml	85ml	85ml	125ml	125ml
eggs (60g)	1	1	1	1	1	2	2
soured cream	1½ tablespoons	60ml	60ml	85ml	85ml	125ml	125ml
baking time (approx)	50 minutes	1 hour	30 minutes	1 hour	45 minutes	1¼ hours	1 hour

Ingredients	deep 20cm round	deep 22cm round	shallow 25cm round	deep 25cm round	deep 30cm round	deep 35cm round
self-raising flour	150g	225g	225g	260g	450g	600g
plain flour	100g	150g	150g	185g	300g	400g
bicarb. of soda	¾ teaspoon	1 teaspoon	1 teaspoon	1¼ teaspoons	2 teaspoons	3 teaspoons
mixed spice	2 teaspoons	3 teaspoons	3 teaspoons	1 tablespoon	2 tablespoons	2 tablespoons
light brown sugar	165g	220g	220g	275g	440g	660g
coarsely grated carrot	480g	720g	720g	900g	1.44kg	1.92kg
vegetable oil	165ml	250ml	250ml	310ml	500ml	665ml
eggs (60g)	3	4	4	5	8	12
soured cream	165ml	250ml	250ml	310ml	500ml	665ml
baking time (approx)	1½ hours	1¾ hours	1¾ hours	2 hours	2½ hours	3¼ hours

Ingredients	shallow 10cm square	deep 10cm square	shallow 15cm square	deep 15cm square	shallow 18cm square	deep 18cm square	shallow 20cm square
self-raising flour	35g	50g	75g	110g	110g	150g	150g
plain flour	2 tablespoons	35g	50g	75g	75g	100g	100g
bicarb. of soda	¼ teaspoon	¼ teaspoon	½ teaspoon	½ teaspoon	½ teaspoon	¾ teaspoon	¾ teaspoon
mixed spice	½ teaspoon	1 teaspoon	1 teaspoon	2 teaspoons	2 teaspoons	2 teaspoons	2 teaspoons
light brown sugar	2 tablespoons	55g	75g	110g	110g	165g	165g
coarsely grated carrot	120g	180g	240g	360g	360g	480g	480g
vegetable oil	1½ tablespoons	60ml	85ml	125ml	125ml	165ml	165ml
eggs (60g)	1	1	1	2	2	3	3
soured cream	1½ tablespoons	60ml	85ml	125ml	125ml	165ml	165ml
baking time (approx)	40 minutes	1 hour	50 minutes	1¼ hours	1 hour	1½ hours	1 hour

Ingredients	deep 20cm square	shallow 22cm square	deep 22cm square	shallow 25cm square	deep 25cm square	deep 30cm square
self-raising flour	225g	225g	260g	260g	450g	600g
plain flour	150g	150g	185g	185g	300g	400g
bicarb. of soda	1 teaspoon	1 teaspoon	1¼ teaspoons	1¼ teaspoons	2 teaspoons	3 teaspoons
mixed spice	3 teaspoons	3 teaspoons	1 tablespoon	1 tablespoon	2 tablespoons	2 tablespoons
light brown sugar	220g	220g	275g	275g	440g	660g
coarsely grated carrot	720g	720g	900g	900g	1.44kg	1.9kg
vegetable oil	250ml	250ml	310ml	310ml	500ml	665ml
eggs (60g)	4	4	5	5	8	12
soured cream	250ml	250ml	310ml	310ml	500ml	665ml
baking time (approx)	1¾ hours	1 hour	2 hours	1¾ hours	2½ hours	3¼ hours

Ingredients	deep 18cm heart shaped	deep 15cm octagonal	deep 20cm octagonal	12-hole muffin tin (80ml)
self-raising flour	110g	110g	225g	150g
plain flour	75g	75g	150g	100g
bicarb. of soda	½ teaspoon	½ teaspoon	1 teaspoon	¾ teaspoon
mixed spice	2 teaspoons	2 teaspoons	3 teaspoons	2 teaspoons
light brown sugar	110g	110g	220g	165g
coarsely grated carrot	360g	360g	720g	480g
vegetable oil	125ml	125ml	250ml	165ml
eggs (60g)	2	2	4	3
soured cream	125ml	125ml	250ml	165ml
baking time (approx)	1¼ hours	1¼ hours	1¾ hours	30 minutes

tips We used 7.5cm deep cake tins with straight sides.
• Eggs and soured cream should be at room temperature for best results.
• The cake will keep well for 5 days in an airtight container, or can be frozen for 3 months.

1 Preheat oven to 160°C. Grease and line base and side(s) of cake tin with baking parchment, extending paper 5cm above side(s).
2 Sift flours, soda, spice and sugar into bowl. Add carrot; stir in combined oil, eggs and soured cream (do not over-mix). Spread mixture into tin.
3 Bake cake for the time given in chart. Cover cake with foil halfway through baking if cake is over-browning, or lower the oven temperature by 10–20 degrees if cake is over 20cm.
4 Test cake by inserting a skewer into centre of cake; if cooked, skewer will be clean, if there is cake mixture on the skewer, bake cake a further 10 minutes before testing again.
5 Stand cake in the tin for 10–30 minutes, depending on the size of cake, before turning, top-side down, onto wire rack to cool.

WHITE CHOCOLATE MUD CAKE

Ingredients	deep 10cm round	deep 12cm round	shallow 15cm round	deep 15cm round	shallow 18cm round	deep 18cm round	shallow 20cm round
butter	60g	85g	85g	125g	125g	165g	165g
white eating chocolate	35g	45g	45g	75g	75g	100g	100g
caster sugar	110g	150g	150g	220g	220g	295g	295g
milk	60ml	85ml	85ml	125ml	125ml	165ml	165ml
plain flour	50g	75g	75g	110g	110g	150g	150g
self-raising flour	1 tablespoon	2 tablespoons	2 tablespoons	35g	35g	50g	50g
vanilla extract	¼ teaspoon	¼ teaspoon	¼ teaspoon	½ teaspoon	½ teaspoon	½ teaspoon	½ teaspoon
eggs (60g)	1	1	1	1	1	1	1
baking time (approx)	50 minutes	1 hour	50 minutes	1½ hours	1¼ hours	1¾ hours	1¼ hours

Ingredients	deep 20cm round	deep 22cm round	shallow 25cm round	deep 25cm round	deep 30cm round	deep 35cm round
butter	250g	335g	335g	375g	625g	1kg
white eating chocolate	150g	200g	200g	225g	375g	600g
caster sugar	440g	585g	585g	660g	1.1kg	1.76kg
milk	250ml	375ml	375ml	375ml	625ml	1 litre
plain flour	225g	300g	300g	335g	560g	900g
self-raising flour	75g	100g	100g	110g	185g	300g
vanilla extract	1 teaspoon	1 teaspoon	1 teaspoon	1½ teaspoons	2½ teaspoons	1 tablespoon
eggs (60g)	2	3	3	3	5	8
baking time (approx)	1¾ hours	2 hours	1¾ hours	2½ hours	3½ hours	4½ hours

Ingredients	shallow 10cm square	deep 10cm square	shallow 15cm square	deep 15cm square	shallow 18cm square	deep 18cm square	shallow 20cm square
butter	60g	85g	125g	165g	165g	250g	250g
white eating chocolate	35g	45g	75g	100g	100g	200g	150g
caster sugar	110g	150g	220g	295g	295g	440g	440g
milk	60ml	85ml	125ml	165ml	165ml	250ml	375ml
plain flour	50g	75g	110g	150g	150g	225g	225g
self-raising flour	1 tablespoon	2 tablespoons	35g	50g	50g	75g	75g
vanilla extract	¼ teaspoon	¼ teaspoon	½ teaspoon	½ teaspoon	½ teaspoon	1 teaspoon	1 teaspoon
eggs (60g)	1	1	1	1	1	2	2
baking time (approx)	50 minutes	1 hour	1¼ hours	1¾ hours	1½ hours	1¾ hours	1½ hours

Ingredients	deep 20cm square	shallow 22cm square	deep 22cm square	shallow 25cm square	deep 25cm square	deep 30cm square
butter	335g	335g	375g	375g	500g	750g
white eating chocolate	200g	200g	225g	225g	300g	450g
caster sugar	585g	585g	660g	660g	880g	1.3kg
milk	375ml	375ml	375ml	375ml	500ml	750ml
plain flour	300g	300g	335g	335g	450g	675g
self-raising flour	100g	100g	110g	110g	150g	225g
vanilla extract	1 teaspoon	1 teaspoon	1½ teaspoons	1½ teaspoons	2 teaspoons	3 teaspoons
eggs (60g)	3	3	3	3	4	6
baking time (approx)	2 hours	1½ hours	2½ hours	2 hours	3 hours	4 hours

Ingredients	deep 18cm heart shaped	deep 15cm octagonal	deep 20cm octagonal	12-hole muffin tin (80ml)
butter	165g	165g	335g	250g
white eating chocolate	100g	100g	200g	150g
caster sugar	295g	295g	585g	440g
milk	165ml	165ml	375ml	250ml
plain flour	150g	150g	300g	225g
self-raising flour	50g	50g	100g	75g
vanilla extract	½ teaspoon	½ teaspoon	1 teaspoon	1 teaspoon
eggs (60g)	1	1	3	2
baking time (approx)	1¾ hours	1¾ hours	2 hours	45 minutes

tips We used 7.5cm deep cake tins with straight sides.
• Eggs should be at room temperature for best results.
• The cake will keep well for 1 week in an airtight container, or can be frozen for 3 months.

1 Preheat oven to 160°C. Grease and line base and side(s) of cake tin with baking parchment, extending paper 5cm above side(s).
2 Combine chopped butter, broken chocolate, sugar and milk in a saucepan; stir over low heat until mixture is smooth. Transfer mixture to a bowl; cool 15 minutes.
3 Whisk in sifted flours, extract and lightly beaten eggs. Pour mixture into tin.
4 Bake the cake for the time given in chart. Cover cake with foil halfway through baking if the cake is over-browning, or lower the oven temperature by 10–20 degrees if cake is over 20cm.
5 Cake will develop a thick sugary crust during baking (cracks are normal); test for firmness by touching with fingers about 5 minutes before the end of baking time, then, test with a skewer. If cooked, skewer will be clean, if there is cake mixture on the skewer, bake cake a further 10 minutes before testing again. Cool cake in tin.

DARK CHOCOLATE MUD CAKE

Ingredients	deep 10cm round	deep 12cm round	shallow 15cm round	deep 15cm round	shallow 18cm round	deep 18cm round	shallow 20cm round
butter	85g	125g	125g	175g	175g	225g	225g
plain chocolate	135g	185g	185g	270g	270g	360g	360g
instant coffee granules	1½ teaspoons	2 teaspoons	2 teaspoons	3 teaspoons	3 teaspoons	1 tablespoon	1 tablespoon
water	60ml	85ml	85ml	125ml	125ml	165ml	165ml
light brown sugar	55g	75g	75g	110g	110g	165g	165g
plain flour	50g	75g	75g	110g	110g	150g	150g
self-raising flour	1½ tablespoons	2 tablespoons	2 tablespoons	35g	35g	35g	35g
eggs (60g)	1	1	1	1	1	2	2
coffee-flavoured liqueur	1½ tablespoons	2 tablespoons	2 tablespoons	60ml	60ml	60ml	60ml
baking time (approx)	1½ hours	1¾ hours	1½ hours	2 hours	1½ hours	2 hours	2 hours

Ingredients	deep 20cm round	deep 22cm round	shallow 25cm round	deep 25cm round	deep 30cm round	deep 35cm round
butter	395g	430g	430g	525g	900g	1.5kg
plain chocolate	625g	675g	675g	840g	1.5kg	2.5kg
instant coffee granules	1½ tablespoons	1½ tablespoons	1½ tablespoons	2 tablespoons	15g	20g
water	250ml	310ml	310ml	375ml	665ml	1 litre
light brown sugar	220g	275g	275g	330g	585g	880g
plain flour	225g	260g	260g	300g	525g	900g
self-raising flour	50g	75g	75g	75g	150g	200g
eggs (60g)	3	4	4	4	7	12
coffee-flavoured liqueur	85ml	85ml	85ml	125ml	250ml	335ml
baking time (approx)	2½ hours	2¾ hours	2¼ hours	3¼ hours	4¼ hours	5 hours

Ingredients	shallow 10cm square	deep 10cm square	shallow 15cm square	deep 15cm square	shallow 18cm square	deep 18cm square	shallow 20cm square
butter	60g	110g	125g	225g	225g	395g	395g
plain chocolate	90g	180g	185g	360g	360g	625g	625g
instant coffee granules	1 teaspoon	2 teaspoons	2 teaspoons	1 tablespoon	1 tablespoon	1½ tablespoons	1½ tablespoons
water	1½ teaspoons	85ml	85ml	185ml	185ml	250ml	250ml
light brown sugar	2 tablespoons	75g	75g	165g	165g	220g	220g
plain flour	2 tablespoons	75g	75g	150g	150g	225g	225g
self-raising flour	1 tablespoon	1½ tablespoons	2 tablespoons	35g	35g	50g	50g
eggs (60g)	1	1	1	2	2	3	3
coffee-flavoured liqueur	1 tablespoon	1½ tablespoons	2 tablespoons	60ml	60ml	85ml	85ml
baking time (approx)	1¼ hours	1¼ hours	1¾ hours	2¼ hours	2 hours	2½ hours	2¼ hours

Ingredients	deep 20cm square	shallow 22cm square	deep 22cm square	shallow 25cm square	deep 25cm square	deep 30cm square
butter	430g	430g	525g	525g	750g	1kg
plain chocolate	675g	675g	840g	840g	1.2kg	1.7kg
instant coffee granules	1½ tablespoons	1½ tablespoons	2 tablespoons	2 tablespoons	10g	15g
water	310ml	310ml	375ml	375ml	560ml	750ml
light brown sugar	275g	275g	330g	330g	495g	660g
plain flour	260g	260g	300g	300g	450g	600g
self-raising flour	75g	75g	75g	75g	110g	150g
eggs (60g)	4	4	4	4	6	8
coffee-flavoured liqueur	85ml	85ml	125ml	125ml	185ml	250ml
baking time (approx)	2¾ hours	2¼ hours	3¼ hours	3 hours	3¾ hours	4¾ hours

Ingredients	deep 18cm heart shaped	deep 15cm octagonal	deep 20cm octagonal	12-hole muffin tin (80ml)
butter	225g	225g	430g	395g
plain chocolate	360g	360g	675g	625g
instant coffee granules	1 tablespoon	1 tablespoon	1½ tablespoons	1½ tablespoons
water	185ml	185ml	310ml	250ml
light brown sugar	165g	165g	275g	220g
plain flour	150g	150g	260g	225g
self-raising flour	35g	35g	75g	50g
eggs (60g)	2	2	4	3
coffee-flavoured liqueur	60ml	60ml	85ml	85ml
baking time (approx)	2 hours	2 hours	2¾ hours	45 minutes

tips We used 7.5cm deep cake tins with straight sides.
• Eggs should be at room temperature for best results.
• We used a good quality plain eating chocolate for this recipe.
• Use soft light brown sugar in this recipe, not soft dark brown or raw sugar.
• The cake will keep well for 1 week in an airtight container, or can be frozen for 3 months.

1 Preheat oven to 160°C. Grease and line base and side(s) of cake tin with baking parchment, extending paper 5cm above side(s).
2 Combine chopped butter, broken chocolate, coffee, the water and sugar in saucepan; stir over low heat until smooth. Transfer mixture to bowl; cool 15 minutes.
3 Whisk in sifted flours, lightly beaten eggs and liqueur. Pour mixture into tin.
4 Bake cake for the time given in chart. Cover cake with foil halfway through baking if cake is over-browning, or lower the oven temperature by 10–20 degrees if cake is over 20cm.
5 Cake will develop a thick sugary crust during baking (cracks are normal); test for firmness by touching with fingers about 5 minutes before the end of baking time, then, test with a skewer. If cooked, skewer will be clean, if there is cake mixture on the skewer, bake a further 10 minutes before testing again. Cool cake in tin.

FRUIT CAKE

Ingredients	deep 10cm round	deep 12cm round	shallow 15cm round	deep 15cm round	shallow 18cm round	deep 18cm round	shallow 20cm round
mixed dried fruit	175g	250g	250g	350g	350g	650g	650g
marmalade	2 teaspoons	3 teaspoons	3 teaspoons	1 tablespoon	1 tablespoon	1½ tablespoons	1½ tablespoons
dark rum	1½ tablespoons	2 tablespoons	2 tablespoons	60ml	60ml	85ml	85ml
butter	60g	90g	90g	125g	125g	160g	160g
finely grated citrus rind	½ teaspoon	¾ teaspoon	¾ teaspoon	1 teaspoon	1 teaspoon	1½ teaspoons	1½ teaspoons
dark brown sugar	55g	75g	75g	110g	110g	165g	165g
eggs (60g)	1	1	1	2	2	3	3
plain flour	75g	110g	110g	150g	150g	225g	225g
mixed spice	¼ teaspoon	¼ teaspoon	¼ teaspoon	½ teaspoon	½ teaspoon	¾ teaspoon	¾ teaspoon
baking time (approx)	1¼ hours	2 hours	1½ hours	2½ hours	1¾ hours	2½ hours	2¼ hours

Ingredients	deep 20cm round	deep 22cm round	shallow 25cm round	deep 25cm round	deep 30cm round	deep 35cm round
mixed dried fruit	750g	1kg	1kg	1.5kg	2.2kg	3kg
marmalade	1½ tablespoons	2 tablespoons	2 tablespoons	60ml	5 tablespoons	125ml
dark rum	85ml	125ml	125ml	185ml	310ml	335ml
butter	200g	250g	250g	375g	625g	800g
finely grated citrus rind	1½ teaspoons	2 teaspoons	2 teaspoons	2 teaspoons	1 tablespoon	1½ tablespoons
dark brown sugar	165g	220g	220g	330g	550g	660g
eggs (60g)	3	4	4	6	10	12
plain flour	250g	300g	300g	450g	750g	1kg
mixed spice	1 teaspoon	1 teaspoon	1 teaspoon	1½ teaspoons	2½ teaspoons	1 tablespoon
baking time (approx)	3 hours	3½ hours	3 hours	4 hours	6 hours	7 hours

Ingredients	shallow 10cm square	deep 10cm square	shallow 15cm square	deep 15cm square	shallow 18cm square	deep 18cm square	shallow 20cm square
mixed dried fruit	175g	250g	350g	650g	650g	750g	1kg
marmalade	2 teaspoons	3 teaspoons	1 tablespoon	1½ tablespoons	1½ tablespoons	1½ tablespoons	2 tablespoons
dark rum	1½ tablespoons	2 tablespoons	60ml	85ml	85ml	85ml	125ml
butter	60g	90g	125g	160g	160g	200g	250g
finely grated citrus rind	½ teaspoon	¾ teaspoon	1 teaspoon	1½ teaspoons	1½ teaspoons	1½ teaspoons	2 teaspoons
dark brown sugar	55g	75g	110g	165g	165g	165g	220g
eggs (60g)	1	1	2	3	3	3	4
plain flour	75g	110g	150g	225g	225g	250g	300g
mixed spice	¼ teaspoon	¼ teaspoon	½ teaspoon	¾ teaspoon	¾ teaspoon	1 teaspoon	1 teaspoon
baking time (approx)	1 hour	2 hours	2¼ hours	2½ hours	2¼ hours	3 hours	3 hours

Ingredients	deep 20cm square	shallow 22cm square	deep 22cm square	shallow 25cm square	deep 25cm square	deep 30cm square
mixed dried fruit	1kg	1kg	1.5kg	1.5kg	2.2kg	3kg
marmalade	2 tablespoons	2 tablespoons	60ml	60ml	5 tablespoons	125ml
dark rum	125ml	125ml	185ml	185ml	310ml	335ml
butter	250g	250g	375g	375g	625g	800g
finely grated citrus rind	2 teaspoons	2 teaspoons	2 teaspoons	2 teaspoons	1 tablespoon	1½ tablespoons
dark brown sugar	220g	220g	330g	330g	550g	660g
eggs (60g)	4	4	6	6	10	12
plain flour	300g	300g	450g	450g	750g	1kg
mixed spice	1 teaspoon	1 teaspoon	1½ teaspoons	1½ teaspoons	2½ teaspoons	1 tablespoon
baking time (approx)	3½ hours	3¼ hours	4 hours	3¾ hours	5 hours	6½ hours

Ingredients	deep 18cm heart shaped	deep 15cm octagonal	deep 20cm octagonal	12-hole muffin tin (80ml)
mixed dried fruit	650g	650g	1kg	750g
marmalade	1½ tablespoons	1½ tablespoons	2 tablespoons	1½ tablespoons
dark rum	85ml	85ml	125ml	85ml
butter	160g	160g	250g	200g
finely grated citrus rind	1½ teaspoons	1½ teaspoons	2 teaspoons	1½ teaspoons
dark brown sugar	165g	165g	220g	165g
eggs (60g)	3	3	4	3
plain flour	225g	225g	300g	250g
mixed spice	¾ teaspoon	¾ teaspoon	1 teaspoon	1 teaspoon
baking time (approx)	2½ hours	2½ hours	3½ hours	45 minutes

tips We used 7.5cm deep cake tins with straight sides.
• Butter and eggs should be at room temperature for best results.
• Use equal amounts of lemon and orange rind.
• Cooling cakes upside down will make them sit flat and level for decorating.
• Cake will keep well at room temperature if wrapped in cling film and stored in an airtight container; or freeze, wrapped in cling film in an airtight container.

1 Preheat oven to 150°C. Grease and line base and side(s) of tin.
2 Mix fruit, marmalade and rum in bowl. Beat butter, rind and sugar in another bowl with electric mixer until combined; beat in eggs, one at a time. Stir butter mixture into fruit mixture; stir in sifted flour and spice. Spread mixture into tin. Tap tin firmly on work top to settle mixture, level top of cake with wet spatula.
3 Bake cake for the time given in chart. Cover cake with foil halfway through baking if cake is over-browning, or lower the oven temperature by 10–20 degrees if cake is over 20cm.
4 Feel surface of cake; it should feel firm. Remove from oven, close oven door, gently push blade of a sharp-pointed knife through centre of cake, right to base of tin. Withdraw knife slowly, feel blade with your fingers; if you feel uncooked mixture, return cake to oven for another 15 minutes before testing again. If the blade is free from mixture, the cake is cooked through.
5 Immediately the cake is cooked, cut off paper around edge(s) of tin. Turn cake, in tin, upside-down onto foil; wrap cake and tin tightly with foil. Cover with a towel; cool completely upside-down.

READY-MADE ICING

This is a great product and very forgiving for the amateur cake decorator. As with anything, you will get better at handling the icing with practice. It's available in 500g packets from supermarkets (usually found amongst the baking goods), and some health-food shops and delicatessens and is found in much larger quantities from cake decorating shops.

We have specified the amount of this icing you will need for each recipe. We have presumed you have initially covered the cake with either almond paste, ganache or a thin layer of ready-made icing (page 120), so we have specified only enough ready-made icing to make a thin layer over the initial covering. Should you want to use ready-made icing as the only covering on a cake, you will have to triple the quantity called for in each recipe. In most cases, cakes covered with this icing need to be left to dry for about 2 days – the time depends on the weather. If the weather is humid or wet and the icing is not drying out, put the cake in a small room, such as a bathroom or laundry, with a fan heater. Don't have the fan too hot or blowing directly onto the cake, just in case there is dust in the heater. The hot air will soon dry out the icing. Some cakes in this book need to be decorated with the ready-made icing unset so patterns can be imprinted on it; others require it to be firm or completely set. Follow individual recipe instructions.

Colouring ready-made icing: Use good quality food colourings for best results (not the liquid dyes found in supermarkets). Always start with a tiny dab of the colouring (use a skewer or toothpick), work it through a small ball of the icing with your fingers until it is evenly coloured. Determine the depth and strength of the colouring before adding any more and kneading it through the rest of the icing. Some cake decorating suppliers stock ready-made icings already coloured – this saves a lot of time and effort.

To cover a cake with ready-made icing: Brush the initial covering on the cake well, and evenly, with sugar syrup before you roll out the icing. Cut off as much icing as you need; re-wrap the remaining icing to exclude air or a crust will develop, which will spoil the smooth texture of the icing. Knead icing, working colouring in, on a surface dusted lightly with a little cornflour until icing is smooth and loses its stickiness. Then use a little cornflour on both the work surface and your hands, to handle the icing when rolling it out. It's important you don't use too much cornflour, as it will dry out the icing, which will cause cracks to occur in the icing when you cover the cakes. Cover any rolled icing with cling film or a vinyl mat while not working with it to prevent it from drying out. Roughly measure up the side of the cake, across the top and down the other side so you have an idea of how large to roll the icing (the icing will stretch once you pick it up and while you're

Dab a little colouring onto the icing with a toothpick. Knead on a lightly cornfloured surface to work the colouring through evenly.

Roll out the icing on a lightly cornfloured surface. Roll from centre to the outside edge turning and easing the icing to fit cake.

Gently roll icing around rolling pin. Hold the pin with one hand while supporting the icing with the other. Lift icing over cake.

placing it over the cake). Use your hand to press the icing out first to a manageable thickness in the shape of the cake (circle, square), then start rolling from the centre of the icing outwards; don't roll over the edge of the icing. Use a rolling pin to roll the icing to the correct size and thickness (about 3-4mm, for the final cover). The icing can be rolled between sheets of baking parchment, or use a non-stick mat that's suitable for rolling out icing. The mats can be bought from cake decorating shops. When rolling, try to keep the icing the shape you need, to match the shape of the cake, and the same thickness all over; do this by gently stretching and rotating the icing around as you roll. Never turn the icing over when rolling it out. Roll the icing around the rolling pin, then lift the icing over the cake. Dust your hands lightly with cornflour, and mould and smooth the icing around the shape of the cake, gently easing out any folds in the icing. Make sure the icing feels as if it is clinging to the cake and there are no air pockets under the icing. Using plastic smoothing tools, smooth the edges and corners of the cakes neatly. Use a small sharp pointed knife to carefully trim away excess icing from around the base of the cake. Scraps of icing will keep well for months if they're wrapped tightly in cling film to exclude the air. If you're making a tiered cake, incorporate the scraps into the next batch of icing. If air bubbles develop in the icing during kneading, use a fine pin or fine needle to burst the bubbles, then gently smooth the icing with your fingers. The bubble and the hole from the pin will soon disappear.

HOME-MADE ICING

If you really want to make your own icing (often referred to as fondant), it's easy to make, but not as easy as buying it.

3 teaspoons powdered gelatine
2 tablespoons water
2 tablespoons glucose syrup
2 teaspoons glycerine
500g icing sugar

1 Combine gelatine, the water, glucose and glycerine in a small saucepan. Stir over medium heat, without boiling, until gelatine is dissolved. Remove from the heat; cool until liquid is barely warm.
2 Meanwhile, finely sift icing sugar into a medium bowl. Add warm liquid; stir until mixture becomes too stiff to stir.
3 Use your hand to work ingredients into a ball, then turn the icing onto a surface dusted with more sifted icing sugar. Knead icing until smooth. Enclose icing in cling film to keep airtight.

makes 500g
tips Keep icing at a cool room temperature for 2 days, or in the fridge for 1 week. It can also be frozen for 3 months; thaw overnight in the fridge.
• Knead icing on a surface dusted lightly with cornflour to return it to its correct consistency.

Lower the icing onto cake surface, unrolling it from the rolling pin at the same time. The icing will stretch a little at this stage.

With lightly cornfloured hands, quickly smooth top of cake, then smooth sides, easing the icing around the shape of the cake.

Trim excess icing from base of cake. Burst any air bubbles with a fine pin. Using smoothing tools, smooth icing. Neaten cake base.

PREPARING CAKES FOR COVERING WITH READY-MADE ICING

It's important cakes are properly prepared before icing. A poor covering means the cake won't stay fresh for long, and bacteria may contaminate the cake, degrading both the cake and the icing, not to mention affecting those who eat it. The cakes will keep for up to 2 weeks if covered correctly with an initial layer of ganache or almond paste, then finally covered with ready-made icing so it is airtight. Fruit and mud cakes, if covered and stored correctly, will keep for longer than other cakes. Cupcakes and smaller or cut cakes, will only keep a couple of days. The cakes must be stored in a dust-free area at a cool room temperature.

Trimming cakes: Cakes must first be trimmed before any covering is applied. Most cakes need some trimming to make them flat and a good shape for decorating. We found by cooling heavy cakes, such as mud and fruit cakes, upside-down, their own weight flattens them, and this should minimise trimming. A cake needs to sit flat and level on its board, and is almost always turned top-side down to cover with icing. After the cake has cooled and the lining paper removed, turn the cake top-side up and, using a large serrated knife, cut enough from the top so that it sits flat when turned top-side down. Use a ruler and a small spirit level to get the cake as flat as possible; it's well worth the effort. .

Securing cakes to boards: After trimming, cakes need to be secured to their boards so they can be carried safely. Royal icing anchors the cakes well, but if you're not using it to decorate the cakes, then a walnut-sized piece of ready-made icing works well, too. Knead a little cooled boiled water or sugar syrup (page 123) into the icing until it is soft and spreadable. Spread icing into the centre of the board then position the cake on the icing. Leave to dry out and set -- it will hold the cake securely within about 24 hours.

Patching cakes: Once secured to the board, patch any large holes in the cake's surface – this mainly applies to fruit cakes. Use tiny balls of ready-made icing or almond paste to fill the holes (page 122); smooth level using a metal-bladed spatula before initially covering with either almond paste, ganache or ready-made icing.

Initial covering: We prefer to use ganache or almond paste for the initial covering. Alternatively, you can use one thick layer of ready-made icing, in which case, triple the quantities used. After the cake is trimmed, secured and patched, it is ready for the initial covering.

Initial covering with almond paste: If a cake is to be covered with almond paste, first brush it with sugar syrup or warmed sieved jam (page 123). This helps the paste stick to the cake. The almond paste should be brushed again with syrup prior to the final covering of ready-made icing.

Initial covering with ready-made icing: You can use a thin layer of ready-made icing (about 2mm thick) under another thin layer of ready-made icing; brush the cake with sugar syrup before applying the initial layer, then brush that layer with syrup before applying the second (final) layer.

Initial covering with ganache: Apply the initial covering of ganache very thinly, then, if covering with ready-made icing, brush the ganache with sugar syrup so the icing sticks.

Use a large sharp serrated knife to cut the rounded top off the cake so that it will sit flat when turned upside-down.

Turn the trimmed cake upside-down; position on the royal icing as soon as it's been applied to the board. Wriggle cake into position.

ROYAL ICING

All cake decorators mainly use royal icing for piping. It's easy to make, but a little harder to achieve the right consistency for whatever you're using it for. Using royal icing for piped flowers requires the stiffest consistency; while piping dots and lines etc, requires the softest consistency; piping shells, stars, basket weave and leaves etc, needs a medium consistency. The amount of icing sugar to use is determined by the size of the egg white and the consistency required. Getting the icing just right is a matter of experience.

We use an electric mixer for the quantity given in our recipe. Smaller quantities can be mixed in a cup using a teaspoon. A teaspoon, or even less, of egg white is good to work with, especially for finer piping. Cake decorators often make royal icing by hand as this gives good results and minimises the development of air bubbles.

It's most important to keep this icing away from the air, as it soon develops a crust, making it unusable for piping – tiny bits of crust will block the piping tubes.

Cover the surface of the icing closely with cling film, then a damp cloth, just to be sure.

ROYAL ICING

240g icing sugar, approximately
1 egg white
¼ teaspoon strained lemon juice

1 Sift the icing sugar through a fine sieve.
2 Lightly beat the egg white in a small bowl with an electric mixer until mixture is just broken up – do not whip into peaks. Beat in the icing sugar, a tablespoon at a time, to get the required consistency.
3 When icing reaches the right consistency, mix in the juice using a wooden spoon.

tips Beat the egg whites slowly, just to break them up. You don't want to turn them into meringue, or add air bubbles – air bubbles are hard to get rid of and will affect the look of your icing and the way it comes out of the piping tube. An air bubble can cause a piped line of icing to break.

• Sifting icing sugar with a very fine sieve is important, as any tiny lumps will block fine piping tubes.
• If properly covered and sealed, royal icing will keep at a cool room temperature or in the fridge for several days. Beat it with a wooden spoon to bring it back to the correct consistency. Keep a wooden spoon aside just for beating royal icing. Regularly-used wooden spoons absorb fat, and the last thing you need in royal icing is any trace of fat.
• You can buy a royal icing mix from cake decorating suppliers; this works well and is very convenient to use.

Colouring royal icing: Because royal icing is white it will take on any colouring. Good quality colourings are expensive, but they are concentrated, so a little goes a long way. They are also quite stable – the colour usually doesn't change much on standing. Use a toothpick or a skewer to dab a little colouring onto the icing. Mix through with a wooden spoon, regularly scraping down the side of the bowl.

Beat egg white on low speed in a small bowl; gradually add sifted icing sugar. Beat until combined; do not whisk into peaks.

When icing reaches the desired consistency, use a wooden spoon to stir in the juice and to break up any large air bubbles.

Cover surface of icing closely with cling film, then a damp cloth, to exclude air and to prevent a crust from forming on the icing.

ALMOND PASTE

Almond paste, often referred to as marzipan or marzipan paste, is the traditional undercoat for rich fruit cakes, which are then usually covered with ready-made icing. Almond paste is easy to make, however, it can be bought ready-made from cake decorating suppliers, some health-food shops, delicatessens, supermarkets and specialty food shops; price is a good guide to quality.

Ideally, almond-paste covered cakes need to stand for at least one day (depending on the weather – longer if the weather is humid) at room temperature to set (dry) before they are covered with ready-made icing. This gives a firm, manageable surface for the final layer. Roll out the paste on a surface lightly dusted with sifted pure icing sugar.

Covering cakes with almond paste: Trim and level the top of the cake, so it will sit flat on the board (page 120). Secure the cake to the board, top-side down. Use tiny balls of almond paste to patch any large holes in the surface of the cake; smooth the paste with a small metal-bladed spatula. Roll thin ropes of almond paste, thick enough to fill any gaps where the cake joins the board; gently push the paste around and under the base of the cake to fill any gaps, then smooth the paste with a spatula.

There are two methods for covering cakes with almond paste. Cakes 20cm or less are easily covered with one large piece of almond paste. Larger cakes are better covered using strips of almond paste for the side(s), and a square, rectangular or round shape cut to size, to cover the top of the cake. Brush sugar syrup over cake before covering.

To cover a large cake: To cover the sides of the cake, measure up the side of the cake to determine its height then around the cake. Brush the cake all over with sugar syrup. Roll a piece of paste into a long strip, trim to fit around the side(s) of the cake; do this in about four batches, depending on the size of the cake. Position the strips of paste around the side(s) of the cake. If you like slightly rounded corners on a square or rectangular cake, wrap strips of paste around the corners, joining strips somewhere along the side of the cake. If you prefer sharper corners, take the strips to the corner edge, use your fingers to mould the joins together at each corner.

To cover the top of the cake, use the base of the cake tin as a guide, and roll out a piece of paste large enough to cover the top of the cake. Use your hands or a rolling pin to lift the paste into position on the cake. Use your fingers to mould the joins together. Smooth the paste with cornfloured hands, then use the smoothing tools to smooth the paste. Using a small sharp knife, trim around the base of the cake to neaten.

Use small pieces of almond paste to fill and patch any holes in the cake's surface; smooth level with the cake, using a metal spatula.

Roll long thin pieces of almond paste thick enough to cover gap around the base where it sits on the board. Smooth with a spatula.

Roll paste on lightly cornfloured surface until large enough to cover cake; lift paste onto cake, smooth icing with hands.

ALMOND PASTE

375g icing sugar
125g ground almonds
2 tablespoons brandy
1 egg yolk
1 teaspoon strained lemon juice

1 Sift icing sugar and ground almonds into a large bowl; discard any lumps. Stir in remaining combined ingredients.
2 When mixture becomes too stiff to stir, use your fingers to press the ingredients together. Turn paste onto surface dusted with extra sifted icing sugar; knead gently until paste becomes smooth and pliable.
3 Wrap paste in cling film to keep airtight until required.

makes 500g
tips Almond paste will keep well in the refrigerator for 2 weeks or frozen for several months. Thaw the frozen paste in the refrigerator overnight.
• If you're covering cakes with almond paste before ready-made icing, you will need the same quantity of almond paste as the ready-made icing specified in the recipe.

SUGAR SYRUP

This can be bought from cake decorating shops, but it's quick, easy and inexpensive to make at home. This is used to brush onto the cake's surface before covering with almond paste, ready-made icing or ganache (to make them stick). The syrup is then brushed over the initial covering before the final layer of ready-made icing, or ganache, is applied.

220g caster sugar
125ml water

1 Combine sugar and water in a small saucepan; stir over high heat, without boiling, until sugar is dissolved.
2 Bring syrup to the boil; boil, uncovered, for 5 minutes without stirring. Cool.
3 Pour syrup into a screw-top jar, store in the fridge for up to 4 weeks.

JAM

Rather than brushing or joining the cakes with sugar syrup, you can use jams, conserves or jellies combined with complementary liqueurs or spirits instead.

As a guide, for a deep 20cm cake you will need 80g jam and 1 tablespoon liqueur. Warm jam in a small bowl over a small saucepan of simmering water; strain the jam while it's warm into another small bowl, then stir in the liqueur.

Alternatively, warm the jam in a microwave safe bowl, strain it, then add the liqueur. Make sure the combinations of flavours marry well with the cake itself.

Here are some ideas:
• Apricot jam and Grand Marnier or Cointreau or limoncello
• Orange marmalade and whisky
• Raspberry or strawberry jam and Framboise
• Plum jam and brandy
• Fig jam and rum or brandy
• Redcurrant jelly and brandy

When the cake feels smooth and even, trim around the base. Use smoothing tools to make the paste as even and flat as possible.

To cover a large cake, 22cm or more (round, square or rectangular), cut manageable strips of paste large enough to cover sides.

Mould the joins together with cornfloured fingers. Use the cake tin as a guide to cut out a piece of paste to cover top of the cake.

BUTTER CREAM

Butter cream is a popular, easy-to-make cake frosting. We've left our recipe unflavoured, but you can use any extract, essence or grated citrus rind to flavour it.

It's important to have the butter at room temperature, not melted or too soft. Use a small narrow mixing bowl, so that the beaters of the electric mixer can get well down into the mixture.

The best way to cover a cake with butter cream is to spread a thin layer all over the cake, then refrigerate the cake to set the butter cream; this will capture any loose crumbs. Apply the remaining butter cream, spreading it as evenly as possible.

Colouring the butter cream:
Butter cream will always have a slightly yellow tinge to it from the butter content. This is quite tricky to counteract, especially if you want to colour it pink, as it is inclined to end up an apricot/salmon colour. You can buy a whitening agent from cake decorating suppliers, which will fix the problem. Beat this in before adding any colouring. Use a skewer or toothpick to dab a tiny amount of colouring onto the butter cream. Use a wooden spoon to mix the colouring through the butter cream evenly before adding any more.

BUTTER CREAM

125g softened butter
240g icing sugar
2 tablespoons milk

1 Beat the butter (and any flavouring, if using) in a small narrow bowl with an electric mixer until the butter is as white as possible. (This will result in a whiter butter cream, which will give you better results when colouring it.)
2 Gradually beat in half the sifted icing sugar, then the milk, then the remaining sifted icing sugar.
3 Beat until the butter cream is smooth and spreadable. Keep scraping down the side of the bowl during beating.

For chocolate butter cream: Sift 35g cocoa powder in with the icing sugar.

makes enough to cover a deep 20cm cake.
tips Coloured butter cream will usually change colour within a few hours. It's a good idea to colour a small amount and let it stand overnight to see what happens. Some colours darken, others become lighter.
• Butter cream will keep for about a week in the fridge. Allow it to come to room temperature before beating it again either with a mixer or a spoon. If it's beaten when it's too cold, it will separate. If this happens, let the mixture come to room temperature, then drain off and reserve the liquid. Beat the remaining butter mixture with an electric mixer until it becomes smooth, then beat in the reserved liquid.
• Cakes covered with butter cream can be stored in the fridge for up to 24 hours. Return cake to room temperature before serving.

Beat the butter in a small narrow bowl with an electric mixer until butter is as white as possible before adding sifted icing sugar.

Gradually beat in half the icing sugar, then the milk, then remaining icing sugar. Beat until the butter cream is spreadable.

Use a skewer or toothpick to dab a tiny amount of colouring onto butter cream. Use a wooden spoon to beat in the colouring.

FLUFFY FROSTING

This frosting can be flavoured with any extract or essence and, because it's so white, it will happily take on any colour. We always stick to pastel colours when we use this frosting. If you want a strong-coloured frosting, however, such as red, this recipe won't work, as you need to add so much colouring that it softens the frosting, and it won't set.

Once all the syrup has been added, beat in the colouring, a tiny dab at a time to control the colour. Scrape down the side of the bowl and the beaters to ensure the colouring is evenly distributed throughout.

We used a sugar thermometer in the recipe, but it's not essential, just boil the sugar syrup until it's thick with heavy bubbles; it should not be coloured. Remove from the heat and let the bubbles subside, then test the thickness by dropping 1 teaspoon of the syrup into a cup of cold water. It should form a ball of soft sticky toffee.

Have the cake ready to be frosted as the frosting will begin to set quite quickly as it cools down. The frosting will be glossy for a few hours, then it will become dull and meringue-like in appearance and taste.

FLUFFY FROSTING

220g caster sugar
80ml water
2 egg whites

1 Stir sugar and the water in a small saucepan over high heat, without boiling, until sugar is dissolved. Boil, uncovered, without stirring, about 5 minutes or until syrup reaches 114°C on a sugar thermometer. Remove from heat, allow the bubbles to subside.
2 Begin to beat the egg whites in a small bowl with an electric mixer on a medium speed towards the end of the syrup's cooking time. Keep beating the egg whites while the sugar syrup reaches the correct temperature, or the egg whites will deflate.
3 With the mixer on medium speed, slowly pour in the hot syrup in a thin, steady stream; if the syrup is added too quickly, the frosting will not thicken. Once all the syrup is added, continue beating on medium to high speed for about 10 minutes or until the mixture is thick and stands in stiff peaks; the frosting should be barely warm at this stage. Use the frosting immediately.

makes enough to cover a deep 20cm cake.
tips Sugar thermometers must be heated to boiling point before placing into boiling syrup, otherwise the thermometer can break. Digital thermometers are easier to use; they are simply placed into the boiling syrup.
• When making syrup, stir sugar and the water over heat until the sugar dissolves; any grains of sugar on the side of the pan should be brushed down into the liquid using a wet pastry brush. When the sugar is dissolved, bring the syrup to the boil; once the syrup is boiling, stop stirring.

Stir the sugar and the water in a pan over high heat until the sugar dissolves. Boil until the temperature reaches 114°C.

Begin to beat the egg whites in a small bowl with an electric mixer towards the end of the cooking time of the syrup.

With the mixer on medium speed, gradually pour the hot syrup into the egg whites in a thin steady stream. Beat until thick.

GANACHE

Ganache is a mixture of melted chocolate and cream. It is wonderfully simple to make and versatile to use. It can be used while it's still warm as a glaze over a cake, or even as a sauce with cake. Or, let the ganache partly set, either at a cool room temperature or in the refrigerator, then beat it with a wooden spoon until it's spreadable – making it a perfect filling or frosting. Ganache can be refrigerated for around 30 minutes, or until it becomes thick and spreadable, then whipped with an electric mixer until it increases in volume and becomes fluffy, making it ideal for a frosting or filling.

Ganache will keep in the refrigerator, covered tightly, for about 2 weeks (stand at room temperature to soften before use), or frozen for 3 months; thaw overnight in the refrigerator, or thaw it in the microwave oven, using short bursts of power.

Chocolate

We used dark- or milk-eating chocolate when testing the ganache recipe, use whichever type you'd be happy to eat and suits the cake. We prefer not to use cooking chocolate, but it will still work in the recipe (right). We don't use high-fat (over 70%) or low-fat chocolate.

Couverture chocolate is expensive, but the results are wonderful. It can be bought at some delicatessens and specialty food stores.

White chocolate deserves a special mention as it can be a little tricky to work with – be very careful not to overheat it or it will 'split' (turn grainy). We found that by adding more chocolate in proportion to the amount of cream (as compared to milk or dark chocolate) we got better results. Also, we found by chopping white chocolate finely, it melted faster and was less likely to split. We broke the chocolate into pieces straight into the bowl of a food processor, then processed it until finely chopped. If the ganache does split, cool it in the refrigerator, then beat the mixture with an electric mixer;

this method hasn't failed us yet. See the finer points of melting chocolate on page 128.

Covering cakes with ganache:

This method of using ganache as the initial covering under ready-made icing will result in a well-shaped cake that will taste good, too.

Make the ganache recipe (right). Level and trim the cake (page 120), and secure it to the board; patch the cake, if necessary (page 122), and brush lightly with sugar syrup (page 123). Spread a very, very thin coating of ganache all over the cake to hold the crumbs in place and to use as a base for the next layer of ganache (or ready-made icing or frosting). Think of this fine ganache layer as an undercoat. Stand ganache at a cool room temperature until firm to touch. (If the cake is firm, and has no crumbs, this undercoat is not necessary.)

If also using ganache as the second covering, once the undercoat is firm, lightly brush the

You can make the ganache by placing the chocolate and cream in a heatproof bowl over a saucepan of simmering water.

The heat from the water will melt the mixture; stir occasionally until smooth. The water should not touch the bottom of the bowl.

Cool ganache in the fridge or at room temperature, stirring occasionally. Beat with an electric mixer until light and fluffy.

cake again with sugar syrup, then use a metal spatula to spread a 1cm layer of ganache over the cake, as evenly as possible. Take your time to get the shape of the cake as perfect as possible; it's worth the effort. Use a straight-sided scraper to smooth the top and side(s) of the ganache covering. Stand the cake at a cool room temperature for about 24 hours, or the until ganache is firm and dry to touch. An air-conditioned room is perfect. If no other covering is to be applied to the ganache-covered cake, it can be refrigerated, if the weather is hot, or stand at a cool room temperature, until needed (up to a week). Bring to room temperature before cutting and serving.

When covering a ganache undercoat with ready-made icing or frosting, brush the ganache lightly, but evenly, with sugar syrup so the next layer will stick. Trim and neaten any rough edges from the surface of the cake so you don't tear the ready-made icing when applying.

note If covering cakes with ganache then ready-rolled icing, the cake should not be refrigerated as the ganache will absorb the moisture from the fridge, and transfer this to the ready-made icing, making it wet to the touch, sticky and it won't hold its shape.

WHITE CHOCOLATE GANACHE

360g white eating chocolate
125ml double cream

1 Break chocolate into food processor, process until chocolate is chopped finely.
2 Bring cream to the boil in a small saucepan; remove from heat.
3 Add chocolate to cream; stir until smooth.
4 Cool mixture to room temperature if not being used as a glaze (in which case use while warm and pourable) before beating or whipping to the desired consistency.

makes enough to cover a deep 20cm round cake.

DARK OR MILK CHOCOLATE GANACHE

200g milk or dark eating chocolate
125ml double cream

1 Bring cream to the boil in a small saucepan; remove from heat.
2 Break chocolate into pan with hot cream; stir until smooth.
3 Cool mixture to room temperature if not being used as a glaze (in which case use while warm and pourable) before beating or whipping to the desired consistency.

makes enough to cover a deep 20cm round cake.

note For a really impressive cake, cut it into layers, as we have done in the step shots, and top the layers with ganache, before covering the cake. You could also layer the cake with butter cream, curd, jam or any type of filling that suits the cake.

When layering a cake, spread each layer with ganache. If the weather is hot, refrigerate the layered cake before completing it.

When covering a firm cake (with no crumbs) with ganache, it doesn't need an undercoat; just spread ganache all over the cake.

Smooth the ganache covering all over with a scraping tool. Take your time to get the shape of the cake as perfect as possible.

CHOCOLATE

There are several ways to melt chocolate, regardless of the colour. We prefer to use a glass, china or ceramic bowl when melting chocolate over a pan of simmering water as these heat slowly, and melt the chocolate gently. Stainless steel bowls also work, but be aware that metal conducts heat rapidly, which can cause the chocolate to overheat if it's not watched carefully.

Seizing: This occurs when water comes in contact with the chocolate, causing it to turn hard and grainy, making it impossible to work with. You will have to start again with another batch of chocolate. It only needs the tiniest amount of water to seize.

Melting in a medium saucepan: Place a medium heatproof bowl over a pan of simmering water; don't let the water touch the base of the bowl as this can overheat the chocolate. Stir occasionally. Remove the bowl from the pan as soon as the chocolate is smooth, to prevent it from overheating.

Melting in the sink: Another easy and mess-free method is to put the chocolate into a bowl – we use a stainless steel bowl. Stand the bowl in a sink of hot tap water, or a larger bowl of hot water. Stir occasionally until the chocolate is smooth. This method takes a little longer, but it's fail-proof. The water should come about half-way up the side of the bowl.

Melting in a microwave: This works a treat if you don't overheat the chocolate. Check your instruction manual for the best way. Usually 50% or 75% power is right for melting chocolate. Place chocolate in a microwave-safe

Melt in a sink Place chocolate in a stainless steel bowl in a sink (or a larger bowl) half-filled with hot tap water; stir occasionally.

Melt over a saucepan Place chocolate in a glass bowl over a pan of simmering water; don't let water touch bowl; stir occasionally.

Melt in a microwave Place in a microwave-safe bowl; heat on medium heat. Stir often, as it holds its shape when melted.

Stir chocolate away from the heat until smooth. Microwaved chocolate will hold its shape, so test by pressing with a spoon.

To make curls Spread melted chocolate thinly, but evenly, onto a cold surface such as marble or stainless steel; allow to almost set.

For long curls, use a sharp long-bladed knife, holding the blade at a 45-degree angle, drag the knife over surface to make curls.

bowl, then microwave it using short bursts of power. Check every 20 seconds by pressing it with a spatula – it could be melted even though it has retained its shape. Don't let the tiniest drop of water near the chocolate or it will seize. Never cover or partially cover the bowl or the chocolate while it's melting, as condensation will form under the lid or covering, and drops of moisture will fall into the chocolate – and it will seize.

Making chocolate curls: There are quite a few ways to make curls, all of which will make different-sized and shaped curls. The classic way is to spread melted chocolate evenly over a cold surface, such as marble,

a stainless steel work top or a flat oven tray; leave it at room temperature until it is almost set – up to 10 minutes. Drag the blade of a large sharp knife, held at about a 45-degree angle, across the chocolate to make curls. It is important the chocolate is at the right stage. If the chocolate is not set enough, it will not curl and if the chocolate is set too much, the curls will break.

Another way to make small chocolate curls is to scrape a vegetable peeler along the side of a block of chocolate. A cheese planer is good for larger curls. Make the curls from the back of a whole block of chocolate. Place the block, flat-side up, on a board and place your hand on the

surface to warm it slightly. Drag the planer over the chocolate block. You may have to re-warm the chocolate with your hand several times during the process.

If you want large chunky curls, spread melted chocolate onto a cold surface and drag an ice-cream scoop across the surface of the almost-set chocolate.

Piping chocolate: A small paper piping bag (page 131) is the best for piping chocolate. Snip a tiny tip off the end and pipe messages or shapes directly onto a cake, or onto baking parchment – the chocolate dries quickly and can be lifted straight onto the cake. Always pipe more than you need as breakages will occur.

For short chunky curls (1) Allow the melted chocolate to almost set then hold the tip of an ice-cream scoop on the surface.

For short chunky curls (2) Firmly drag the ice-cream scoop over the surface of the chocolate using an even pressure.

For large curls Soften back of bar by holding your hand on the surface for about a minute. Drag cheese planer across chocolate.

For smaller curls Slightly warm the chocolate block; drag the blade of a sharp vegetable peeler evenly down the side.

To pipe chocolate (1) First make a paper piping bag (page 131), then half-fill the bag with melted chocolate; fold over top of bag.

To pipe chocolate (2) Snip a tiny tip from the piping bag. With bag at a 45-degree angle, pipe freehand or use a pattern.

MODELLING PASTE

Many different shapes can be made using this paste. It's easy to make and keeps for several days at room temperature, wrapped in cling film. It can be bought in cake decorators' shops, however, we use home-made paste as the shapes dry and stay firmer longer.

Modelling paste can be moulded into 3D shapes, such as animals or people, which can then be wired to stand up on the cake. The paste can also be rolled out thinly, and cutters used to cut out petals and other shapes. Petals are often dried separately, then assembled into buds and flowers by using royal icing to secure petals together, or by wiring the petals together with floral wire.

Work with small amounts of paste only, as once it's exposed to air it dries out quickly. Cling film is perfect for enclosing pieces of paste to keep it airtight. Most cut-out shapes need further shaping, so keep pieces under cling film, or a piece of vinyl, until you're ready to use them. Finished shapes need to be dried out. This takes varying amounts of time depending on the weather and the thickness of the paste. As a guide, thin petals will dry in a few hours; more solid shapes, such as letters 1cm thick, may take 2 days to dry out completely.

Many shapes are wired and positioned in the cake. For health reasons, don't insert the wired shapes into the cake until the day of the function as, once pierced, the cake's seal is broken and bacteria may enter. A more hygienic way to use flower spikes: these hollow plastic spikes are pushed into the cake and used to hold the decoration in place.

MODELLING PASTE

2 teaspoons powdered gelatine
1½ tablespoons water
2 teaspoons glucose syrup
240g icing sugar

1 Sprinkle gelatine over the water in a heatproof cup; stand cup in small saucepan of simmering water, stir until gelatine is dissolved. Stir in glucose.
2 Sift icing sugar into medium bowl; stir in gelatine mixture then, when mixture becomes too stiff to stir, use your hand to combine the ingredients.
3 Knead on surface dusted with extra sifted icing sugar until smooth and elastic. Wrap tightly in cling film to keep airtight.

makes 250g

Colouring modelling paste:
Since the paste is white it colours easily. Start with a small dab of colouring, applied to a small ball of paste, to determine the strength of the colouring. Once you're happy with the colour, tint the rest of the paste you need.

Shapes made from modelling paste can be painted with food colouring once they're dried out.

Wiring shapes: This must be done as soon as the shape is established. Wire is usually dipped in flower glue and pushed into the shape, then allowed to dry.

FLOWER GLUE

1 tablespoon tylose powder
2 tablespoons water

1 Combine ingredients in a screw-topped jar; shake well, stand overnight (lumps will dissolve overnight).
2 Stir in a little more water to bring to the consistency of unbeaten egg white; shake well.

tips This glue must be made at least 12 hours before using.
• It keeps indefinitely at room temperature, but will thicken on standing. Return it to the consistency of unbeaten egg white by stirring in a little more water each time you use it.

Work the ingredients together. Turn paste onto surface dusted with sifted icing sugar; knead until smooth. Enclose in cling film.

Keep paste covered with cling film or a piece of vinyl to stop it from drying out. Only work with small quantities at a time.

PIPING BAGS & TUBES

Paper piping bags: These are incredibly useful, especially if you're working with different coloured icings in small quantities. They can be used for piping ganache and butter cream as well as royal icing.

You can make your own, using baking or greaseproof paper, though baking parchment is the stronger of the two. You can also buy large paper triangles suitable for making larger piping bags; these are available from cake decorating shops, craft equipment stockists and shops supplying chefs and cooks.

Basic piping used for dots, lines, loops, snail's trails, etc. (page 132), don't really require the use of a piping tube. Half- or three-quarters fill a paper piping bag with royal icing – whichever feels comfortable in your hand. Gently squeeze the icing down to the tip of the bag; fold the top of the bag over to enclose the icing. Using a pair of sharp scissors, snip the tiniest tip from the base of the bag, then do a test run. If the amount of icing that comes out is not suitable, snip another tiny

piece from the bag until you get the opening just right. You can use piping tubes in these bags as well; tubes give you more control over piped icing. If you're using piping tubes, use two thicknesses of baking parchment to make the bags stronger. Follow the steps below to making paper bags: with practice you will become quick at making them in no time.

Disposable plastic piping bags: These can be bought from supermarkets in a useful medium size. You need to use piping tubes with these bags, unless you're doing some simple piped work like dots or writing (in which case, put the icing in the bag and snip the tip from the bag until the opening is of the correct size). Some bags come with a kit of a few plastic piping tubes; while these are good for some piping, they are not suitable for fine work.

Fabric piping bags: These come in a wide range of sizes, from quite small to very large. The small ones are usually used for cake decorating, either with a piping

tube or fitted with a piping screw (also known as a 'coupler'), which secures the piping tube to the outside of the piping bag, making it a simple process to change tubes or to use the tube with a different coloured icing. Larger piping bags are usually fitted with large tubes; these are suitable for piping whipped cream, meringue and butter-based frostings. After use, wash the bags in warm water and leave to dry over a bottle.

Piping tubes: These are available in many sizes, either made from plastic or metal. Metal tubes are more expensive but will last a lifetime. Wash in warm water, using a small paint brush around the tip to clean them thoroughly. Never clean out leftover mixture by poking your finger through the end of the tube, as it can get stuck, which is particularly painful if it's a sharp fluted tube. Smaller diameter tubes and fluted tubes are delicate and can easily become distorted, which will affect the outcome of your piping. So treat your tubes with care and store them properly.

Cut a perfect square from baking parchment, fold it in half diagonally. Use a sharp knife to cut along the fold to make two triangles.

Hold apex of triangle towards you, wrap one point of triangle around to form a cone. Wrap remaining point around to make bag.

Wriggle the points of the triangle together until they line up perfectly. Staple the bag to secure the three points in place.

PIPING TECHNIQUES

To pipe dots *Touch the tip of the tube on the surface with bag upright. Squeeze to make dot, stop squeezing, pull tube straight up.*

To make forget-me-nots using a plain tube *Pipe five dots in a circle, then finish with one dot in the centre of each circle.*

Snail's trail (1) *Using a plain tube, hold bag at a 45-degree angle, touch down with tube squeezing bag to make a teardrop of icing.*

Snail's trail (2) *Gradually reduce pressure on bag, lifting tube slightly. Touch tube on surface, stop squeezing, making a tiny trail.*

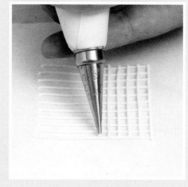

Straight lines (1) *Using a plain tube, hold bag at a 45-degree angle, touch tube down, squeeze bag to make a dot of icing.*

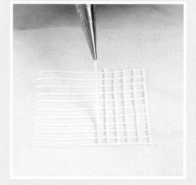

Straight lines (2) *Keep pressure on bag by squeezing gently. Lift tube up from anchor point, piping evenly, towards where it ends.*

Straight lines (3) *Lower tube, slightly reducing pressure on bag, to finish line of icing. If it breaks, let it set, then lift off with a pin.*

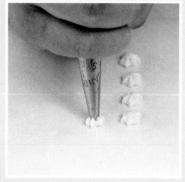

Stars (1) *Using a fluted tube, hold the bag upright, squeeze the bag, keeping tip of tube barely above surface; pipe a star shape.*

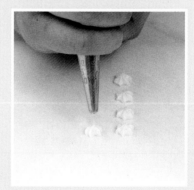

Stars (2) *While tube is barely above surface, gradually reduce, then stop squeezing the bag. Pull tube up without leaving a point.*

We used royal icing and a number 2 plain (writing), number 8 fluted (shell) and number 22 (basket weave) tube on these two pages. Piping is not difficult, it just takes practice.

Shell edging (1) Holding bag at a slight angle, touch tip of fluted tube on surface, squeeze bag. Lift tube slightly to make a shell shape.

Shell edging (2) Gradually reduce pressure on the bag to make a short tail on the shell. Start a new shell shape at the end of the tail.

Rope pattern Using fluted tube, touch tube on surface, squeeze bag while lifting tube and moving it clockwise in a small tight circle.

Feather and fan (1) Hold bag almost upright, touch fluted tube on surface, squeeze bag, and twist tube to pipe a question mark.

Feather and fan (2) Reduce pressure on bag as you pipe to make the tail of the question mark. Repeat on other side.

Candle holders Using fluted tube, touch tip on surface, squeeze the bag while moving the tube in a circular pattern at the same time.

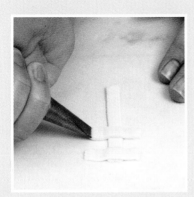

Basket weave (1) Touch tip of basket weave tube on surface, pipe a vertical line. Pipe horizontal lines a tube's width apart.

Basket weave (2) Pipe another vertical line, a tube's width apart from the first, barely covering ends of the horizontal lines.

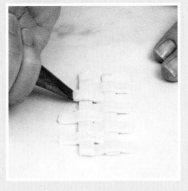

Basket weave (3) Fill in the gaps with piped short horizontal lines. Keep an even pressure on the bag of icing during the piping.

STACKING & SUPPORTING TIERS

Throughout this book we've used quite a lot of tall cakes to get the effect we wanted. Sometimes we needed to stack two deep cakes for a really impressive tall cake, other times one deep and one shallow cake stacked together gave us enough height. When stacking and joining same-sized cakes, always stack the shallow cake on top of the deep cake. The charts on pages 102–117, listing eight different cake choices, will give you the recipes for making the correct-sized cakes. You can buy the cakes, but make sure you buy deep cakes, or you might have to stack three shallow cakes to achieve the height.

Joining uniced cakes: Cakes can be joined using either jam or ganache. Use any jam you like to join the cakes, one that will complement the flavour of the chosen cake or cakes (page 123). Sometimes it's pleasantly surprising to mix and match two or three different-flavoured cakes. If joining different-flavoured cakes, attach each cake to its own board (page 137), so that the cakes are easy to separate at serving time using a long-bladed metal spatula.

Trim the tops of the cakes to be joined, so they will sit flat on each other (page 120). Join the cut surfaces of the cakes with jam or ganache to minimise any crumbs escaping. Secure the cake to the board (page 120).

Once joined to the board(s), patch the cakes, if necessary (page 122); brush with sugar syrup and apply the initial covering of almond paste, ready-made icing or ganache and dry overnight or until dry to touch. Apply the second (final) layer to the cakes and leave overnight or until dry (this may take 2 days). You are now ready to support and stack the cakes.

Supporting tiers: Thick wooden skewers are used to support the weight of the upper tiers. Measure the diameter of the board under the next cake tier. Lightly mark this area in the centre of the tier below. (This is to ensure the next tier is centred on top of the bottom tier, otherwise the weight of the tiers will not be evenly distributed, which can cause heavy cakes to tilt and look unbalanced.) Insert the skewers, pointy end down, right through to the cake board about 1cm in from the marked area to make neat holes in the bottom cake.

Remove the skewers, then push them into the same holes, blunt-side down, through to the board. Mark each skewer level with the surface of the cake tier (note which skewer came from which hole). These skewers will support the next tier, so it's important to have no gaps where the tiers join. Use a hacksaw, strong secateurs or a strong serrated knife to cut the skewers as straight as possible, so they are level with the top of the cake tier. Push the skewers into their correct position, cut-side down. (It's best to do this one skewer at a time, so that each skewer is returned to its original hole.)

Push pointed ends of skewers into centre of cake right through to touch the board, keeping them straight. This makes a neat hole.

Remove the skewers, one at a time, then push back into the cake, blunt-side down. Mark the skewers close to the cake surface.

Use a serrated knife to cut skewer at the mark; discard pointed end. Replace skewer into cake. It's best to do one skewer at a time.

Repeat the skewering process with all the tiers, except the top tier. We use three skewers for each round cake and four skewers for each square cake between each tier. Skewers can be inserted into uniced cakes, if they are to be stacked then iced (cakes must be on boards if using skewers).

Stacking cakes: Once the skewers have been inserted into the cakes, the tiers can be stacked on top of each other. Stack and secure the next tier onto the centre of the cake below with royal icing or ready-made icing softened with some cooled boiled water. Carefully sit the next tier of the cake on top of the skewers, pressing down gently to secure the bottom of the cake board to the iced cake below. Continue stacking all the tiers in the same way, being careful not to damage the covering when skewering and stacking. Fill any gaps between the tiers, where the cakes join the boards.

Filling any gaps: If a cake is to be covered with ganache or a similar frosting, gaps will be easy to cover. If the cakes are covered with ready-made icing, sometimes decorations or an edging around the tiers will cover any small gaps. To fill larger gaps, and keep the cake airtight, tint some royal icing the same colour as the icing covering the cake, and pipe a line of icing around the cake; use your finger to blend the icing around the cake.

At serving time, remove the top tier of the cake by sliding a long metal-bladed spatula under the board to remove it from the tier below. Remove all the skewers when cutting and serving the cake.

note: Except for the bottom cake, which is positioned on a board that is 10cm–15cm larger than the cake (or, if being displayed on a cake stand or plate, should be positioned on a board of similar size), each tier is positioned on a wooden board

that is the same size as the cake. This is to minimise any gaps between the tiers – these boards should not be visible at all.

Transporting cakes: Tiered cakes can be very heavy – especially if fruit or mud cakes are used. Often it takes two people to carry a stacked tiered cake (and one to direct where you're walking and positioning the cake). Transporting a tiered cake can be a problem – it's large, it's heavy and you'll need to anchor the cake for its journey in the car (do not transport it on the car seat). A thin piece of sponge rubber is usually enough to hold the cake still. Allow plenty of headroom for the cake. The only other way of handling and transporting multi-tiered cakes is to assemble the tiers at the venue. This is often impractical to do.

Use a spatula to spread a dollop of royal icing (or softened ready-made icing) over the centre of the cake, covering the skewered area.

Position the next cake tier, on its board, on the icing before it sets. Centre the cake by wriggling it into position. Dry overnight.

To cover any gaps, colour royal icing to match cake icing. Pipe icing around base of cake, use fingertip to blend icing into gaps.

CAKE TINS

CHOICE OF CAKE TINS

Cake tins come in all shapes and sizes. Square, rectangular and octagonal shaped tins etc, with straight corners, are better to work with when decorating, as the cakes start off well-shaped.

Cake tins are made from various metals; good-quality heavy tin and aluminium conduct heat evenly. Flimsy tins or those with a non-stick surface can produce cakes with a thick crust – to counter this, reduce the oven temperature by 10–20 degrees.

Make sure you wash and dry tins thoroughly after use – drying them in a low oven is a good idea. They can develop rust if they're not dried properly after use.

Many cake decorating shops will hire cake tins, and this is a good option if you're making a one-time-only cake.

PREPARING CAKE TINS

All cake tins must be either greased, greased and floured, or lined to ensure the cakes don't stick. If the recipe requires a long baking time, it's vital to line the tin correctly to insulate the cake, protect the top of the cake from over-browning and to retain the shape of the cake to minimise patching and trimming, especially if the cake is to be iced and decorated.

Large cakes, over 20cm, round or square, usually need to be baked in lined tins. The larger the cake, the more lining paper required. For added insulation, use a layer of brown paper against the side(s) of the tin, and then line with baking parchment. As a guide, use one layer of baking parchment for cakes that take less than 2 hours to bake, and three layers for cakes that take 2–4 hours. Use a layer of brown paper and three layers of baking parchment (or greaseproof paper) for cakes needing longer than 4 hours to bake.

Lining rectangular, square, octagonal, round or oval cake tins: Cut strips of baking parchment, long enough to encircle the inside of the tin, overlapping the ends slightly, and wide enough to extend 5cm above the side(s) of the tin. Allow for a fold-over at the base. Fold 2cm of the paper over, snip, on an angle, up to the fold, making cuts about 1½cm apart. Lightly grease the inside of the tin with cooking-oil spray or melted butter to hold the paper in place. Position the paper around the side of the tin with the snipped fold at the base. Using the tin as a guide, trace around the base on baking parchment. Cut out paper, cutting slightly inside the marked line to allow for the thickness of the tin. Neatly position the paper in the tin, covering the snipped paper.

Preparing unusual-shaped tins: Some unusual-shaped tins can't be lined efficiently. In this case, grease the tin lightly, but evenly, with melted butter, then refrigerate or freeze the tin. Sprinkle a little plain flour all over the greased area, tap and turn the tin so that all the butter is lightly coated with flour. Turn the tin upside down over the sink or bin and knock out any excess flour. If you prefer, line the base of the greased tin with baking parchment, then just grease and flour the side(s).

Lightly grease the tin to hold the lining paper in place. Position the paper around the side of the tin, with snipped fold at the bottom.

Trace the tin base onto paper. Cut paper out slightly inside the marked circle. Position in the tin, to cover snipped paper.

Lining a square or rectangular tin is the same as for a round one. Trace the tin base onto paper; position over snipped paper.

CAKE BOARDS

If the cake is to be displayed on a stand, you may need to re-think the size of the base board; consider this before starting to decorate the cake.

Covered boards can be purchased from cake decorating shops. If you want to cover your own, choose a covering that is non-absorbent; cake decorating shops normally supply this type of paper.

Covering rectangular or square boards: Cut the covering paper

To cover a square board, place the board on the back of the covering paper, fold sides of paper over neatly; secure with glue or tape.

To cover a board with ready-made icing, use a pastry brush to evenly coat a paper-covered board with sugar syrup (page 123).

about 5cm larger than the board. Place the board, top-side down, on the back of the paper. Use tape or craft glue to stick the paper to the board. If the paper is thick, cut the corners of the paper as if covering a book. Glue a piece of paper to the back of the board to neaten the appearance.

Covering round boards: Cut the covering paper about 5cm larger than the board. Place the board, top-side down, on the back of

To cover a round board, secure snipped paper to board with glue; glue plain paper to the back of the board to cover snipped paper.

Using rolling pin, cover the board with rolled icing. Smooth with hands and smoothing tools.

the paper. Snip the paper border, on an angle, all the way around. Fold snipped pieces onto the board and tape or glue in place. Glue a piece of paper to the back of the board to neaten the appearance.

Covering boards with ready-made icing: To cover a 30cm board, knead 500g of icing on surface dusted with a little cornflour until icing loses its stickiness. Brush the surface and the side(s) of the board with sugar syrup (page 123). Roll the icing large enough to cover the board, about 3mm thick. Use the rolling pin to lift the icing onto the board; smooth icing using cornfloured hands. Use smoothing tools to gently smooth the icing, easing the icing over the edge(s) of the board. Use a sharp knife to trim the icing neatly around the bottom edge(s) of the board, then smooth the edge with your fingertip (dipped first into cornflour). Stand board for 3 hours or overnight, or until the icing is firm and dry.

Using a sharp knife, trim excess icing from edge of board; smooth edge(s) with fingertips.

MAKING BOWS

Sewing a tailored bow (1) Fold a length of ribbon to make four loops. Stitch in the centre of bow to hold loops together.

Sewing a tailored bow (2) Sew a small strip of ribbon into position in the centre of the bow to cover and neaten the looped ribbon.

Gluing a tailored bow (1) Loop a length of ribbon bringing ends into the centre. Glue into position using a glue gun or craft glue.

Gluing a tailored bow (2) Loop a smaller length of ribbon, secure ends in centre with glue. Glue smaller loop onto larger loop.

Gluing a tailored bow (3) Glue a small strip of ribbon over the centre of the double bow to cover and neaten the middle of the bow.

Tying a simple bow (1) Make two loops from a length of ribbon. Leave enough for tails – make these as long as you want them.

Tying a simple bow (2) Cross the loops over; bring the top loop under bottom loop then through the hole under the bottom loop.

Tying a simple bow (3) Pull the tops of the loops at the same time to make the bow even and roughly the size you want it to be.

Tying a simple bow (4) Wriggle the loops of the bow until they are the same length, and the bow and its centre are as you want them.

CAKE PATTERNS

LATTE LACE CAKE
(page 60)

second
tier

top tier
(larger)

third tier
(smaller)

fourth
tier

bottom tier (left)
(see page 140 for right side)

CAKE PATTERNS

LATTE LACE CAKE
(page 60)

bottom tier (right)

BUCKLE UP BABY CAKES
(page 92)

BRIDAL MOSAIC
SQUARES
(page 78)

GLOSSARY

almonds

ground nuts are powdered to a coarse flour-like texture.

paste similar to marzipan, but is less granular and contains less sugar (*see also* marzipan).

baking parchment silicone-coated paper primarily used for lining baking tins and trays so cakes and biscuits don't stick.

baking powder raising agent consisting of two parts cream of tartar to one part bicarbonate of soda.

ball tool plastic stick with a ball of different sizes at either end. Used to thin ready-made icing when making flower petals, and to smooth curves and rounded ends. There are a number of sizes available.

bicarbonate of soda used as a leavening agent in baking.

blossom cutters tiny cutters used to make small flowers; come as 3, 4 or 5 petals.

brushes artist's paint brushes and make-up brushes are excellent when brushing cakes, models, flowers and decorations with glitter, powder or dusts, or painting colours, water or sugar syrup onto cakes. Larger-sized brushes are also useful for brushing crumbs off cakes or dried icing from boards.

cachous also known as dragées; these edible tiny (3mm to 5mm) metallic-looking confectionery balls are available in silver, gold or various colours.

cake boards come in myriad sizes, usually round or square and covered in a thick non-absorbent paper, silver or gold in colour. If displaying on a cake board, the base board is often 10–15cm larger than the cake, so it can be lifted and transported easily. The remaining tiers are placed on cake boards of the same size. If displaying on a cake plate, the base board should be the same size as the cake.

chocolate

dark eating made of a high percentage of cocoa liquor, cocoa butter, and a little added sugar.

Melts small discs of compound milk, white or dark chocolate ideal for melting and moulding.

milk mild and very sweet; similar in make-up to dark but with the addition of milk solids.

white contains no cocoa solids but derives its sweet flavour from cocoa butter. Very sensitive to heat so watch carefully when melting.

cocoa powder dried, unsweetened, roasted and ground cocoa beans.

coconut

chips dried, flaked coconut flesh; available raw and toasted.

desiccated dried, unsweetened, finely shredded coconut.

essence produced from coconut flavouring, oil and alcohol.

shredded strips of dried coconut.

cornflour often used as a thickener, here we use it to roll out ready-made icing and modelling paste.

cutters come in many sizes, shapes and styles. Used to cut ready-made icing and modelling paste into different shapes.

edible dust, glitter, powders, shimmer available from cake decorating suppliers. Used to add details and highlights to cakes.

embossing tools these are pressed or rolled onto soft ready-made icing leaving a print of the design. Textured mats are also a type of embossing tool.

floral wire also known as florist's or craft wire. A covered flexible wire that comes in different thicknesses. The higher the gauge number, the finer the wire and the finer the wire the more delicate and flexible it is (used for smaller pieces); the lower the gauge number, the thicker the wire (used for making large sugar flowers). Also used to bind petals when making flowers, or to position shapes or flowers into cakes. The wire itself may be uncovered or wrapped in white or green florist's tape. Available from craft and cake decorating suppliers in cut lengths (36cm) and on spools. When we ask for a length of wire, we mean 36cm lengths.

florist's tape from craft and cake decorating suppliers. Wrapped around flower stems to provide a seal when placing fresh flowers on cakes. Also used to cover wooden dowels, or to cover floral wire when making flowers from modelling paste, etc., to hold petals in place.

flower cutters used to cut small flower shapes (see blossom cutters).

flower mat also known as foam pad. Provides a soft surface when working with ready-made icing and modelling paste to make flower petals, etc. Also provides a soft base when pushing cutouts out of plunger cutters.

flower spikes hollow plastic spikes that are used to position wired flowers and other decorations, thus keeping the floral wire out of the cake. This is a safe, hygienic way to add embellishments to the cake. Fresh flowers can also be positioned in spikes; add a couple of drops of water into the spike to keep the flowers fresh.

food colourings dyes used to change the colour of foods.

concentrated pastes the easiest to use, though these are a little more expensive.

liquid dyes the strength varies depending on the quality. Useful for pastel colours only, as adding large amounts of liquid colouring will break down most icings. Also useful for painting icing sculptures.

powdered colourings best for primary colours or black.

frilling tool usually comes as part of a 'modelling' kit. Used to frill the edges of ready-made icing.

ganache mixture of melted chocolate and cream.

gelatine thickening agent; available in sheet form, known as leaf gelatine, or as a powder. 3 teaspoons of powdered gelatine (7g or one sachet) is roughly equivalent to four gelatine leaves. We used powdered gelatine throughout this book.

glucose syrup clear, thick liquid often made from wheat or corn starch.

glycerine sweet, colourless liquid that retains moisture and adds sweetness to cakes. It also softens ready-made and royal icings.

marzipan almond and sugar paste used to cover cakes, as a filling in pastries or sculpted into a variety of shapes to be used as cake decorations. After kneading, it has the consistency of dough and can be rolled, shaped, cut or moulded (*see also* almond paste).

metal spatula also known as a palette knife. Come in small, medium and large. The larger ones have flexible steel blades. There are two types, straight-bladed, and offset or crank, which is used for getting into tight areas.

mixed fruit mixture of sultanas, raisins, currants, mixed peel and sometimes glacé cherries.

mixed spice blend of ground spices usually consisting of cinnamon, allspice and nutmeg.

modelling paste also known as pastillage. Sets very hard, and is used to make all types of decorations for cakes.

modelling tools used to draw, frill, shape, imprint, stencil, hollow or cut soft icing when making decorations for cakes. Can be found singly, but are also available in kits.

perspex measures clear rulers that come in different widths; used to cut icing ribbons to specified widths for cakes. Often come in a set of 5 widths.

petal cutters various metal or plastic cutters in the shape of flower petals. Available as a kit for specific flowers, which also include the veining tool.

piping bags
disposable bags made of clear plastic. Discard after each use. Available in one size from supermarkets.

paper piping bags made from baking parchment and discarded after each use. Used for small amounts of icing, writing, flooding, etc. See page 131 for directions on how to make them.

polyester bags lightweight, flexible and reusable. Wash in hot soapy water after each use and dry, standing over a soft drink bottle. Available in many different sizes.

piping tubes small metal or plastic cone shapes with various openings used to produce many different designs when icing or frosting is pressed through them. Smaller tubes are quite fragile and must be treated carefully, otherwise they can be bent or squashed out of shape.

plunger cutters have a plunger on top: push to cut the shape, then push to release the cut shape. Will not damage the shape as it pushes it out.

polystyrene tightly-packed foam that resists moisture. Available in different-shaped blocks from cake decorating and craft supply stores.

powders and dusts also known as petal, pearl, sparkles, blossom tints and lustres.

ready-made icing also known as ready-to-roll icing, fondant icing, sugar paste and soft icing. Sweet tasting icing with a dough-like consistency when kneaded. Used to cover cakes and make decorations. Roll on a surface dusted lightly with cornflour; don't use too much cornflour, as the icing will dry and crack when lifted over the cake.

rolling pins come in a variety of sizes; use large ones to roll out the icing, use medium and smaller ones to thin out icing for decorations. They can be made of wood, granite, non-stick plastic, etc.

royal icing mixture of egg white and icing sugar; best to use when securing cakes to their boards. Instant mixes (just add water) are available from cake decorating suppliers.

scrapers can be either plastic or metal. Used to scrape excess ganache from sides of cake, or to remove excess royal icing from stencils. Plastic scrapers are useful when cleaning up, to scrape any icing stuck to the bench top.

skewers used to support the cake tiers. They are not the same as the skewers used in kebabs, etc., they are much thicker so are able to support the weight of the cakes. They are pointed at one end to push all the way through the cake before cutting down to size.

smoothers plastic paddles with handles used to smooth ready-made icing, and remove air bubbles. When smoothing icing you need to use two plastic paddles together; they give the cake a smooth, shiny, appearance.

stamens used to make flower centres; most often sold double-ended, which are either cut in half before using, or are pulled through a hooked wire and folded up in a bunch. May also be found single-ended.

sugar
brown a very soft, fine sugar retaining molasses for its flavour.
caster finely granulated table sugar.
icing granulated sugar crushed to a powder; sift well before use.

sugar confetti small discs of coloured crunchy sugar.

sugar pearls small round confectionery balls with a shimmer coating.

sugar syrup is brushed all over the surface of a cake before applying the initial covering of ganache, almond paste or ready-made icing. It sticks the initial covering layer to the cake and sticks the final layer to the initial layer. It also stops the cake from drying out.

textured mats see embossing tools.

tylose powder when mixed into royal icing, almond paste, ready-made icing or modelling paste, it creates a strong paste that dries very hard. Used when something is required to set in a certain position.

vanilla
pod the tiny black seeds impart a luscious vanilla flavour.
extract obtained from vanilla pods infused in water.

veining tool also known as a leaf veiner. Plastic moulds that leave an imprint of a leaf when pressed on ready-made icing. Available in kits along with matching flower petal cutters.

wooden dowels or dowel rods, used to support cakes over three tiers so they can be transported safely. Cut with a small hacksaw to the size required (just below the height of the cake).

INDEX

CONVERSION CHARTS

measures

One metric tablespoon holds 20ml; one metric teaspoon holds 5ml.

All cup and spoon measurements are level. The most accurate way of measuring dry ingredients is to weigh them. When measuring liquids, use a clear glass or plastic jug with metric markings.

We use large eggs with an average weight of 60g.

dry measures

METRIC	IMPERIAL
15g	½oz
30g	1oz
60g	2oz
90g	3oz
125g	4oz (¼lb)
155g	5oz
185g	6oz
220g	7oz
250g	8oz (½lb)
280g	9oz
315g	10oz
345g	11oz
375g	12oz (¾lb)
410g	13oz
440g	14oz
470g	15oz
500g	16oz (1lb)
750g	24oz (1½lb)
1kg	32oz (2lb)

liquid measures

METRIC	IMPERIAL
30ml	1 fluid oz
60ml	2 fluid oz
100ml	3 fluid oz
125ml	4 fluid oz
150ml	5 fluid oz
190ml	6 fluid oz
250ml	8 fluid oz
300ml	10 fluid oz
500ml	16 fluid oz
600ml	20 fluid oz
1000ml (1 litre)	32 fluid oz

length measures

3mm	⅛in
6mm	¼in
1cm	½in
2cm	¾in
2.5cm	1in
5cm	2in
6cm	2½in
8cm	3in
10cm	4in
13cm	5in
15cm	6in
18cm	7in
20cm	8in
23cm	9in
25cm	10in
28cm	11in
30cm	12in (1ft)

oven temperatures

These are fan-assisted temperatures. If you have a conventional oven (ie. not fan-assisted), increase temperatures by 10–20°.

	°C (CELSIUS)	°F (FAHRENHEIT)	GAS MARK
Very low	100	210	½
Low	130	260	1–2
Moderately low	140	280	3
Moderate	160	325	4–5
Moderately hot	180	350	6
Hot	200	400	7–8
Very hot	220	425	9

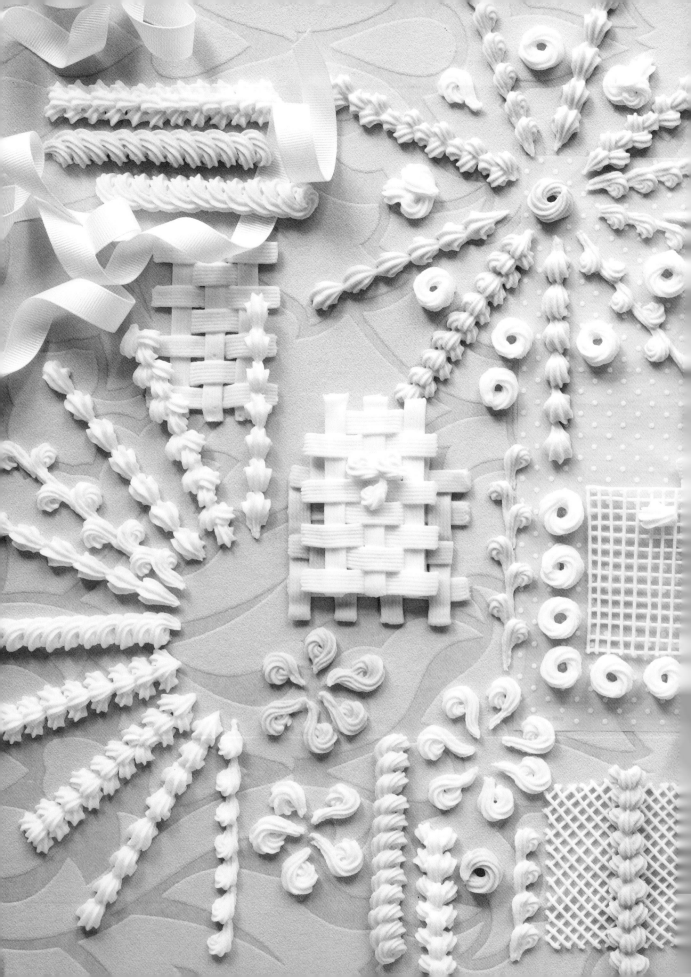